Dandelion Diaries:

A Leadership Blueprint for Marginalized Leaders

LeAnne Salazar Montoya, PhD
Author and Editor

© Salazar Creations, 2025

Table of Contents

A Leadership Blueprint for Marginalized Leaders 1

Dedication 7

Foreword 8

How to Use This Book 13

Chapter 1 15

Planting the Seeds 15

The Call to Leadership 15

Chapter 1 16

Planting the Seeds – The Call to Leadership 16

- The Leadership Calling: Defining Your "Why" 16
- Overcoming Self-Doubt and Imposter Syndrome 16
- Building Your Leadership Identity 17
- Recognizing and Breaking Through Barriers 17
- Blueprint for Success: Crafting Your Leadership Philosophy & Profile 18
- The Seeds You Plant Today Will Become the Leaders of Tomorrow 18

Chapter 2 20

Breaking Through Concrete – Overcoming Systemic Barriers 20

Racial and Gender Disparities in Leadership Roles 20
- Key Research on Leadership Disparities 20

Bias in Hiring and Promotion in Educational Leadership 21
- Key Findings on Bias in Leadership Hiring 21
- Key Research on Hiring Biases 22

Challenges in the Leadership Pipeline for Underrepresented Groups 22
- Strategies for Systemic Change 23

Chapter 3 27

Rooting in Strength – Building a Leadership Foundation 27

- Developing Your Leadership Identity and Philosophy 27
- Building a Modern, Competitive Resume for Leadership Roles 28
- Researching Where You Apply: Understanding the Landscape 29
- Developing Your 90-Day Entry Plan for Leadership Success 30

  Blueprint Task: Crafting Your Leadership Profile 31

  Building Your Leadership Future 31

Chapter 4 33

Cultivating Connections – Relationships, Networks, and Allies 33

  Leadership is Not a Solo Journey..33

Building and Sustaining Professional Relationships 33

  The Power of Mentorship and Sponsorship 33

Leveraging Networks and Affinity Groups 34

  The Role of Affinity Groups in Leadership Development..................................35

Engaging Community Stakeholders for Leadership Success 36

  The Role of Community Engagement in Educational Leadership 36

Building a Leadership Ecosystem 37

Chapter 5 39

Weathering the Storms – Navigating Challenges with Grace 39

  The Resilient Leader..39

Leading Through Adversity and Crisis...39

  Key Leadership Strategies for Crisis Management..39

Managing Conflict and Difficult Conversations..40

  Best Practices for Managing Conflict as a School Leader 40

Balancing Advocacy with Diplomacy..41

  How to Advocate for Change Without Political Backlash..................................42

Leadership in the Eye of the Storm 42

Chapter 6 45

Blooming in Leadership – Leading with Purpose and Impact 45

  Growing into a Transformational Leader 45

Transformational Leadership Strategies 45

  Four Pillars of Transformational Leadership (Bass & Riggio, 2006) 45

Leading for Equity: Advocacy in Action..46

  Key Components of Equity-Centered Leadership 46

Strengthening Team Culture and Morale 47

  How to Strengthen Team Culture as a Leader 48

Leading with Purpose, Creating Lasting Impact 49

Chapter 7

Seeding the Future – Mentorship and Legacy Building

The True Measure of Leadership is Legacy

Paying It Forward: Lifting Others as You Climb

The Power of Sponsorship and Mentorship in Leadership

Creating Sustainable Leadership Pipelines for Underrepresented Leaders

Addressing the Gaps in Leadership Pipelines

Crafting a Lasting Impact in Education

Three Pillars of Leadership Legacy

The Future of Leadership is in Your Hands

Chapter 8

The Dandelion's Journey – Personal Narratives of Resilient Leaders

The Power of Storytelling in Leadership

Stories from Diverse, Marginalized School Leaders

A Superintendent's Story: Breaking Barriers as a Latina Leader

An Assistant Principal's Story: Leading as a Black Male Educator

A Principal's Story: Overcoming Imposter Syndrome as a First-Generation Leader

Lessons Learned and Advice for Aspiring Leaders

Reflections on Perseverance, Identity, and Empowerment

Your Story is Still Being Written

Chapter 9

Blueprint for Breaking Barriers in Educational Leadership

Step 1: Define Your Leadership Identity and Philosophy

Step 2: Build a Modern, Competitive Resume

Step 3: Research Where You Apply and Develop an Entry Plan

Step 4: Overcome Bias and Build Your Leadership Presence

Step 5: Strengthen Your Leadership Network and Sponsorship

Final Blueprint Task: Your Personal Equity-Driven Leadership Action Plan

📌 Personal Leadership Action Plan

You Belong in Leadership

Chapter 10

Spreading the Seeds – The Next Steps in Leadership

  The Collective Power of Leadership **73**

Encouragement and Next Steps for Readers **73**

A Call to Action for Systemic Change **74**

  How Can You Be a Change Agent in Leadership? 74

What NOT to Do: Avoiding Toxic Leadership Behaviors **74**

Resources and Continued Learning **75**

The Power of Collective Leadership **76**

The Fields We Sow – Leadership, Legacy, and the Power of Representation **76**

  The Work is Not Done, But We Are Not Done Either 77

  The Future is Ours to Shape 77

Appendices **78**

 Leadership Self-Assessment Tool **79**

 Career Planning Template for Aspiring Leaders **80**

 Practice Interview Questions **81**

  Vision & Leadership Style 81

  Strategic Planning & Decision-Making 81

  Equity, Diversity, and Inclusion 81

  Stakeholder Engagement & Communication 82

  Talent Development & Organizational Culture 82

  Your Leadership Journey Begins Today 83

10 Takeaways: The Dandelion's Journey and the Struggle of Marginalized Leaders **84**

About the Author **88**

References **89**

Dedication

This book is dedicated to the **women, the leaders of color, the first-generation professionals, the LGBTQ+ trailblazers, the underrepresented, the underestimated, and the ones who never quite fit the mold**—to those who have had to **fight twice as hard, work twice as long, and endure professional hostility simply because they dared to lead on their own terms.**

To those who have faced **gaslighting, professional hazing, and the weight of systemic exclusion**, who have been told they were "too ambitious," "too emotional," "too inexperienced," or simply "not ready"—know this: **You were always enough.** You were never the problem.

The barriers you've encountered were never about **your capabilities, intelligence, or worth**—they were about **the fragility of those who feared your presence, your power, and your undeniable ability to change the landscape of leadership.** You were never a **"diversity hire,"** nor were you given anything you did not rightfully earn. The real issue has never been about **your qualifications but about breaking the unspoken rules designed to keep you out.**

A professor once told me, "F* imposter syndrome. There is no such thing. There is only fragility among those who feel threatened by our breakthroughs."** Those words have stayed with me, and I pass them on to you. **You belong here. You always have.**

Like the **dandelion**, you have pushed through concrete, endured the harshest conditions, and yet you bloom—unapologetically, beautifully, and resiliently. Your success is not just **a personal victory**—it is a seed of hope, a challenge to the status quo, and a call for the next generation to rise with even greater strength.

May you continue to **take root, flourish, and spread your leadership far and wide.** The field is yours to grow.

"WE ARE NOT WEEDS IN THE GARDEN OF LEADERSHIP—WE ARE THE DANDELIONS THAT BREAK THROUGH CONCRETE, UNSHAKEN BY RESISTANCE, SPREADING SEEDS OF CHANGE WHERE THEY ONCE SAID WE DID NOT BELONG."

– DR. LEANNE SALAZAR MONTOYA

Foreword

Leadership is not just about reaching the top—it is about **creating space for others, transforming systems, and ensuring that schools reflect the diverse voices and experiences of their communities.** Yet, for many aspiring leaders—particularly women and leaders of color—the path to educational leadership is filled with **barriers, biases, and systemic challenges.**

DANDELION DIARIES is a **blueprint for those who have been overlooked, underestimated, or told to wait their turn.** It is for the **teacher who is ready to step into administration but lacks mentorship,** the aspiring principal who needs **strategic guidance to navigate the hiring process,** and the **experienced leader who is pushing against the limitations of systemic inequities.** This book offers **step-by-step guidance, real-world strategies,** and **practical blueprints** to help you secure and excel in leadership roles—**regardless of the obstacles in your way.**

Whether you are **preparing for your first leadership role** or seeking to **advance in your career,** this book provides the tools to help you **define your leadership identity, position yourself for success, and create a lasting impact in your schools and communities.**

The Significance of Dandelions as a Symbol of Resilience, Adaptability, and Leadership

The **dandelion** is often dismissed as a **weed,** but in reality, it is one of the most **resilient and adaptable plants in nature.** It grows in the harshest conditions—**breaking through concrete, thriving in unlikely places, and spreading its seeds far and wide.**

Much like the dandelion, **marginalized leaders** often rise in environments that do not initially welcome them. They **push through systemic barriers, challenge the status quo, and redefine what leadership looks like. The seeds they plant— through mentorship, advocacy, and transformational leadership—carry forward, creating change long after they have moved on.**

This book embraces the **dandelion as a metaphor for leadership**—not the traditional, carefully cultivated leadership that follows prescribed pathways, but **the bold, disruptive, and necessary leadership that emerges in unexpected places.** It is a reminder that **you do not need permission to lead**—you only need the will to **grow, adapt, and take up space.**

Personal Reflection on the Leadership Journey

My journey into leadership was not **linear, traditional, or easy.** As a **first-generation scholar from rural New Mexico**, I did not see many leaders who looked like me at the table. There was no **roadmap** for navigating **bias, limited opportunities, or the unspoken rules that govern educational leadership.** I had to **learn by doing, advocate for myself, and create opportunities where none existed.**

Over the years, I have **coached, mentored, and championed** countless aspiring leaders—women, educators of color, and those who have been told that their **time hasn't come yet.** I have seen **talented, equity-driven educators** passed over for promotions, struggling to navigate hiring systems designed to **exclude rather than uplift.**

That is why this book exists.

DANDELION DIARIES is **a structured guide to everything I have learned, taught, and lived as a leadership coach.** It is a **written extension of the coaching I provide in person**, giving readers a tangible **step-by-step process to claim their place in leadership.**

As you move through these chapters, you will:
- Clarify your leadership identity and philosophy
- Strategically position yourself for advancement
- Navigate hiring and promotion processes with confidence
- Develop an entry plan to succeed in your first 90 days
- Overcome bias, build networks, and lead with impact

This book is not just about **getting a job**—it is about **creating systemic change** by ensuring that **leadership reflects the diversity, brilliance, and strength of the educators who serve our students every day.**

How to Use This Book

Each chapter will provide:

📖 **Research-Based Insights** – Understanding the systemic barriers in educational leadership
🔍 **Practical Strategies** – Actionable steps to navigate hiring, promotion, and leadership challenges
🌱 **Blueprints for Success** – Templates, prompts, and exercises to apply directly to your leadership journey

At the end of each chapter, you will build a **Leadership Blueprint**, creating a **personalized plan** that you can use as you apply for positions, prepare for interviews, and step into leadership roles.

- **In Chapter 1,** we will start with **planting the seeds of leadership**—defining your "why," overcoming self-doubt, and building the mindset needed to thrive in leadership.

- **In Chapter 2,** we will confront **systemic barriers** and explore strategies to break through hiring biases and inequities.

- **In Chapter 3,** we will focus on **building a leadership foundation,** including crafting a **modern resume, researching where you apply, and developing an entry plan for your first leadership role.**

- **In later chapters,** we will explore **relationship-building, navigating adversity, leading with authenticity, and building a legacy that extends beyond your tenure.**

You are not just preparing for a **position**—you are preparing to **lead with impact.**

The seeds of leadership are already within you. **Now, let's cultivate them together.**

💡 **Next Step:** Turn the page, start your blueprint, and begin the work of stepping into the leadership role you were meant for.

Chapter 1
Planting the Seeds
The Call to Leadership

Chapter 1

Planting the Seeds – The Call to Leadership

The Leadership Journey Begins

Leadership is a calling. For many, it begins with an internal whisper—a realization that they have more to offer, that they see a need for change, and that they are ready to step forward. For marginalized leaders, however, this whisper is often drowned out by doubt, systemic barriers, or the absence of visible role models who have walked the same path. The first step in leadership is not just about deciding to pursue a position—it is about acknowledging your worth, owning your strengths, and choosing to lead with purpose.

This chapter is about planting the seeds of leadership. It will guide you through defining your "why," recognizing your potential, and confronting the fears that might be holding you back. Before we discuss resumes, applications, and interviews, we must first answer the most critical question: **Why do you want to lead?**

The Leadership Calling: Defining Your "Why"

Every great leader has a driving force, a personal mission that fuels their leadership journey. Maybe you want to create opportunities for students who have been overlooked. Perhaps you have seen ineffective leadership and know that you can do better. Or, you might have had a mentor who inspired you to take the next step. Whatever your reason, defining your "why" is essential because it will anchor you during challenges and guide your decision-making as a leader.

Reflection Questions:

What moment made you realize you wanted to be a leader?
What changes do you hope to bring to your school or district?
How does leadership align with your personal values and experiences?

Your "why" is your foundation. It will shape your leadership philosophy, influence the types of positions you apply for, and provide resilience in difficult times.

Overcoming Self-Doubt and Imposter Syndrome

Many aspiring leaders—especially those from underrepresented backgrounds—struggle with **imposter syndrome**, the feeling that they are not "enough" or that they need more experience, more degrees, or more validation before stepping into leadership. The truth is, no one is ever 100% "ready" for leadership. Growth happens through experience, and every leader starts somewhere.

Key Strategies for Overcoming Self-Doubt:

- **Reframe your mindset:** Instead of asking, "Am I ready?" ask, "How can I grow into this role?"

- **Recognize your value:** Schools and districts need diverse leadership—your lived experiences are an asset.

- **Seek affirmation:** Find mentors and colleagues who see your leadership potential and reinforce your strengths.
- **Take action:** The best way to combat doubt is by stepping forward. Apply for the job. Take the interview. Learn from the experience.

If you have been waiting for a sign to step into leadership, **this is it**.

Building Your Leadership Identity

Leadership is not just about what you do—it is about **who you are**. As you prepare for the next steps in your career, it is important to think about the kind of leader you want to be.

Consider the following leadership styles:

- **Transformational Leaders** inspire change and innovation.
- **Servant Leaders** prioritize the needs of their team and community.
- **Instructional Leaders** focus on teaching and learning improvement.
- **Distributive Leaders** believe in shared leadership and collaboration.

Which style resonates most with you? Understanding your leadership identity will help you align with positions and environments that reflect your values and strengths.

Recognizing and Breaking Through Barriers

Marginalized leaders often face unique challenges in the leadership pipeline. Systemic biases, lack of representation, and limited access to mentorship can create obstacles. However, these challenges are not insurmountable. Recognizing the barriers you may face allows you to **strategically prepare** for them.

Common Barriers & How to Overcome Them:
🏃 **Lack of Representation:** Seek out leadership programs and affinity groups (such as ALAS, AERA, and local education networks).
🏃 **Bias in Hiring Practices:** Ensure your resume, application, and interview responses highlight measurable achievements.
🏃 **Limited Access to Mentorship:** Find mentors who can offer guidance, advocacy, and support.
🏃 **Self-Doubt & Burnout:** Prioritize self-care, build a support network, and lean into your "why" when challenges arise.

The fact that you are here—reading this, reflecting on your journey—means you are already pushing past these barriers. You belong in leadership.

Blueprint for Success: Crafting Your Leadership Philosophy & Profile

At the end of this chapter, take time to create your **Leadership Philosophy & Profile**—a personal statement that will guide your career and shape how you present yourself in job applications and interviews.

> **Define Your Why:** What is your purpose in leadership?
> **Describe Your Leadership Identity:** What are your core values and leadership style?
> **List Your Strengths:** What unique experiences and skills set you apart?
> **Identify Areas for Growth:** What skills or knowledge do you want to develop?

This leadership blueprint will serve as your **North Star** throughout your journey. As you move through this book and prepare for your next steps, you will return to this profile again and again to refine and strengthen it.

The Seeds You Plant Today Will Become the Leaders of Tomorrow

Leadership is not just about **getting a job**—it is about **making an impact**. The seeds of leadership you plant today, in defining your purpose, overcoming doubt, and committing to growth, will one day blossom into a career that transforms schools, students, and communities.

You are not just preparing for a leadership position. You are stepping into **a movement**—one that will change education for the better.

Are you ready to lead?

Chapter 2
Breaking Through Concrete
Overcoming Systemic Barriers

Chapter 2

Breaking Through Concrete – Overcoming Systemic Barriers

Despite efforts to diversify educational leadership, **women and people of color remain significantly underrepresented in top leadership roles due to systemic barriers** (Bailes & Guthery, 2020; Fuller & Young, 2022). These barriers manifest in **racial and gender disparities in leadership representation, biases in hiring and promotion, and challenges in the leadership pipeline** that make it difficult for underrepresented groups to ascend to higher positions.

This chapter provides a **comprehensive review of scholarly literature, organizational reports, and empirical research** that explore these barriers and offer **evidence-based strategies for overcoming systemic inequities** in educational leadership.

Racial and Gender Disparities in Leadership Roles

Historically, **educational leadership has been dominated by White and male administrators,** even as the **teaching workforce and student population have grown more diverse** (AASA, 2023; NCES, 2020). Women make up approximately **75% of K-12 teachers,** yet they **remain a minority in superintendent positions** (AASA, 2023). Similarly, **leaders of color remain vastly underrepresented relative to the student populations they serve.**

- **Superintendent Representation:** National data show that **only 26% of district superintendents are women, and only 9% are people of color,** despite **over half of K-12 students identifying as non-White** (AASA, 2023).

- **Principal Representation:** Among school principals, **78% are White, 11% are Black, and 9% are Latino,** highlighting a significant gap between **leadership demographics and student populations** (NCES, 2020).

- **Intersectionality and Barriers for Women of Color:** Women of color face compounded barriers in leadership. **Latinas remain among the most underrepresented and underpaid groups in school leadership,** a disparity that has been consistently documented over the years (Macias & Stephens, 2019).

Key Research on Leadership Disparities

📖 Shakeshaft, C. (1987). WOMEN IN EDUCATIONAL ADMINISTRATION (Sage).

- A **foundational** study that **chronicles the history of women's underrepresentation** in school leadership. It argues that **leadership theories and training models were historically built around male experiences,** leading to systemic exclusion.

📖 Grogan, M., & Shakeshaft, C. (2011). WOMEN AND EDUCATIONAL LEADERSHIP (Jossey-Bass).

- Provides a **modern synthesis of research** on **gender and leadership in education,** examining how **women's leadership styles, career paths, and experiences** differ from those of men. It **advocates for policy and structural reforms** to increase gender equity.

📖 Bailes, L. P., & Guthery, S. (2020). HELD DOWN AND HELD BACK: SYSTEMATICALLY DELAYED PRINCIPAL PROMOTIONS BY RACE AND GENDER (AERA OPEN, 6(2)).

- Analyzing Texas school leadership data, this study found that **even when qualifications were equal, Black and female assistant principals were promoted at significantly lower rates than their White and male peers.** The findings provide **quantitative evidence of systemic disparities in the leadership pipeline.**

📖 Macias, A., & Stephens, S. (2019). INTERSECTIONALITY IN THE FIELD OF EDUCATION: A CRITICAL LOOK AT RACE, GENDER, TREATMENT, PAY, AND LEADERSHIP (JOURNAL OF LATINOS AND EDUCATION, 18(1), 46-64).

- This study highlights **how race and gender intersect to shape leadership experiences,** finding that **Latina administrators face multiple disadvantages, including pay inequity and exclusion from informal leadership networks.**

📖 Cruz, G. (2023). WILL YOUR SCHOOL DISTRICT'S NEXT SUPERINTENDENT BE A WOMAN OR A PERSON OF COLOR? (SCHOOL ADMINISTRATOR, 80(8)).

- Reports that **despite a predominantly female teaching force, men overwhelmingly hold superintendent roles.** The article **references AASA's "The Time Is Now" playbook,** which **provides strategies to increase representation in school leadership.**

Bias in Hiring and Promotion in Educational Leadership

Implicit and explicit biases in hiring and promotion processes **systematically disadvantage women and people of color in school leadership** (Tallerico, 2000; Bailes & Guthery, 2020). These biases **manifest in both overt discrimination and subtle exclusionary practices** that create **barriers to advancement.**

Key Findings on Bias in Leadership Hiring

- **School boards favor male candidates:** Tallerico (2000) found that **hiring committees often undervalue women's leadership skills,** assuming they lack the traits necessary for the superintendency.

- **Delayed promotion for Black and female educators:** Bailes & Guthery (2020) revealed that **Black assistant principals were 18% less likely to be promoted to principal,** and women waited **longer than men** for career advancement.

- **Higher scrutiny and expectations for women:** Macias & Stephens (2019) found that **women were often held to higher performance standards** in hiring and evaluations.

Key Research on Hiring Biases

📖 Tallerico, M. (2000). ACCESSING THE SUPERINTENDENCY: THE UNWRITTEN RULES (Corwin).

- This study **examines how informal selection criteria** (e.g., networking, subjective assessments of "fit") **disadvantage women and candidates of color** in superintendent hiring.

📖 DeMatthews, D., et al. (2023). UNTAPPED TALENT: AN 11-YEAR ANALYSIS OF THE TEXAS SUPERINTENDENT WORKFORCE (2010-2021).

- A **data-driven study** revealing that **women and leaders of color must complete more career steps before becoming superintendents**, while White men more frequently **jump from principal to superintendent without serving in other central-office roles.**

📖 Palmer, B., & Mullooly, J. (2015). PRINCIPAL SELECTION AND SCHOOL DISTRICT HIRING CULTURES: FAIR OR FOUL?(JOURNAL OF EDUCATION & SOCIAL POLICY, 2(2), 26-38).

- A **qualitative study of 221 principals,** finding that many experienced **subjective or biased hiring processes rather than merit-based decisions.**

Challenges in the Leadership Pipeline for Underrepresented Groups

Beyond individual hiring decisions, a **"leaky leadership pipeline"** systematically excludes women and people of color from advancing in school leadership (Fuller & Young, 2022).

- **Fewer leadership development opportunities:** Many women and educators of color report **not being encouraged to pursue leadership** at the same rates as White men (New Leaders, 2022).

- **Lack of sponsorship:** White men are more likely to have **senior sponsors advocating for their promotion,** while women and leaders of color must often **navigate leadership pathways alone** (NAESP, 2024).

- **Pipeline "squeezing out" underrepresented leaders:** Even when **women and people of color enter administration, fewer are promoted,** leading to **whiter and more male-dominated leadership at higher levels**(Bailes & Guthery, 2020).

📖 Fuller, E. J., & Young, M. D. (2022). CHALLENGES AND OPPORTUNITIES IN DIVERSIFYING THE LEADERSHIP PIPELINE(LEADERSHIP AND POLICY IN SCHOOLS, 21(4)).

- This study **maps where BIPOC leaders exit the leadership pipeline,** identifying key points where **structural interventions could improve advancement.**

📖 New Leaders (2022). THE SHOULDER TAP: EDUCATORS OF COLOR ON THE LEADERSHIP REPRESENTATION GAP.

- A national report emphasizing that **mentorship and sponsorship are critical for retaining and promoting diverse school leaders.**

Strategies for Systemic Change

The **lack of diversity in educational leadership is not an individual issue—it is a systemic problem that requires intentional solutions.** Research-backed strategies include:

✔ **Expanding leadership pipelines for educators of color** (Wallace Foundation, 2021).
✔ **Reforming hiring processes to reduce bias** (NASSP, 2023).
✔ **Implementing structured mentorship programs** (New Leaders, 2022).
✔ **Tracking and publicly reporting leadership diversity data** (EdTrust, 2022).

By addressing these challenges with **research-driven policies and leadership development initiatives**, the field of education can **create a leadership landscape that reflects the diversity of the students it serves.**

"Like the dandelion, diverse leaders often bloom in unexpected places—

thriving against odds, spreading resilience, and enriching educational

communities wherever they land."

Dra. LeAnne Salazar Montoya

Chapter 3
Rooting in Strength
Building a Leadership Foundation

Chapter 3

Rooting in Strength – Building a Leadership Foundation

Leadership is not simply about securing a position—it is about knowing who you are, what you stand for, and how you will lead. Many aspiring school leaders from marginalized backgrounds find themselves exceptionally qualified but consistently overlooked in hiring processes (Bailes & Guthery, 2020). The reason often lies not in a lack of ability, but in the failure of traditional hiring systems to recognize diverse leadership strengths (Macias & Stephens, 2019).

The process of stepping into leadership begins long before the interview. It starts with defining your leadership philosophy, crafting a modern and strategic resume, conducting thorough research on prospective positions, and preparing an entry plan that sets you up for success from day one. This chapter will provide clear, actionable steps to help you establish a strong leadership foundation and strategically position yourself for advancement.

By the end of this chapter, you will have a leadership profile that captures your unique vision, skills, and impact, along with an updated resume and research-based job application strategy. Most importantly, you will begin drafting an entry plan—your first 90-day approach to successfully transitioning into leadership.

Developing Your Leadership Identity and Philosophy

Before applying for leadership roles, you need to articulate who you are as a leader. Research shows that candidates who clearly define their leadership philosophy are more likely to advance in the hiring process because they project confidence, clarity, and purpose (Grogan & Shakeshaft, 2011).

Start with a Leadership Philosophy Statement
Your leadership philosophy serves as the guiding framework for how you will lead, inspire, and create change. It should be:

- Clear and concise (3-5 sentences)
- Rooted in your values and lived experiences
- Reflective of your commitment to equity and student success

📌 Example Leadership Philosophy Statement:
"I believe that leadership is about service, advocacy, and transformational change. My purpose as a school leader is to create equitable learning environments where every student has the opportunity to succeed. Through culturally responsive leadership, data-driven decision-making, and community partnerships, I will work to close achievement gaps and foster inclusive school cultures."

Identify Your Leadership Strengths

- Are you an equity-driven leader focused on closing opportunity gaps?
- Do you excel in instructional leadership, driving curriculum and teacher growth?
- Are you a transformational leader, leading school-wide change initiatives?

By understanding your unique strengths, you will be able to effectively communicate why you are the right candidate for leadership roles.

Assess and Address Growth Areas

- Conduct a self-audit using leadership frameworks such as the Wallace Foundation's Principal Standards (Wallace Foundation, 2021).
- Identify gaps in experience or skills and take action (e.g., professional development, mentoring).

This self-awareness will help you tailor your resume, application, and interview responses to showcase your strengths while demonstrating a commitment to growth.

Building a Modern, Competitive Resume for Leadership Roles

The hiring process in education has evolved, and your resume must reflect that evolution. Research has shown that principals and district leaders from underrepresented backgrounds are often subjected to longer hiring delays and additional scrutiny compared to their White and male counterparts (Bailes & Guthery, 2020). This makes it critical to craft a powerful, data-driven resume that immediately demonstrates your impact and readiness for leadership.

Key Elements of a Modern Leadership Resume:
Professional Summary – A strong opening statement that highlights your leadership experience, philosophy, and impact.
Key Achievements – Focus on measurable outcomes (e.g., "Increased student achievement by 22% through targeted intervention programs").
Leadership Experience – Use action-oriented language that showcases your leadership roles.
Certifications & Education – List degrees, administrative licensure, and leadership training programs.
Community and Advocacy Work – Leadership extends beyond the school walls.
Highlight mentorship, committee work, and advocacy efforts.

📌 Example Resume Entry:
Assistant Principal, XYZ Middle School (2018-Present)

- Led equity-focused initiatives that reduced disciplinary referrals for students of color by 30% through restorative justice practices.
- Developed a teacher mentorship program, increasing retention rates by 20% over three years.

- Implemented data-driven instructional strategies, resulting in a 15% increase in reading proficiency among ELL students.

Resume Formatting Tips:

✓ Keep it to 1-2 pages
✓ Use clear, professional formatting
✓ Tailor it for each job posting using relevant keywords

By making these adjustments, your resume will tell the story of your leadership impact, rather than simply listing job descriptions.

Researching Where You Apply: Understanding the Landscape

Before applying for any position, you must conduct strategic research on the district, school culture, and leadership priorities. This ensures that you can:

- Align your application materials with the district's mission and needs.
- Ask informed questions during interviews.
- Position yourself as a leader who understands the specific challenges and opportunities of the district.

Research Strategies:

- Review School & District Reports (NCES, EdTrust, and state education dashboards).
- Analyze School Performance Data (test scores, student demographics, teacher retention rates).
- Read Strategic Plans (to align your leadership vision with district goals).
- Understand School Culture (community forums, board meeting minutes).

📌 Pro Tip: When preparing for interviews, note key district initiatives and think about how your skills and experiences align with them.

Developing Your 90-Day Entry Plan for Leadership Success

Once you secure a leadership position, the first 90 days are critical in setting the tone for your leadership. A well-structured entry plan demonstrates intentionality, preparedness, and strategic thinking—qualities that hiring teams actively seek (Fuller & Young, 2022).

Blueprint for Your 90-Day Entry Plan:

1. First 30 Days: Listen and Learn

   - Conduct stakeholder meetings (teachers, staff, parents, students).
   - Gather qualitative and quantitative data on school culture, instructional practices, and student outcomes.
   - Observe without making immediate changes—build trust.

2. Days 30-60: Assess Strengths and Gaps

   - Analyze school performance data and identify patterns.
   - Engage leadership teams in discussions about needs and priorities.
   - Begin forming preliminary action plans for instructional and operational improvements.

3. Days 60-90: Set Actionable Priorities

   - Communicate a clear vision and first initiatives to stakeholders.
   - Establish quick wins (initiatives that build early momentum).
   - Begin implementing leadership changes with staff buy-in.

📌 Pro Tip: When asked about your leadership approach in an interview, discuss your 90-day entry plan—it will showcase your strategic mindset and preparedness for the role.

Blueprint Task: Crafting Your Leadership Profile

At the end of this chapter, complete the following Leadership Profile Blueprint to refine your identity, strengths, and leadership vision.

📌 Leadership Profile Blueprint

My Leadership Philosophy Statement:

My Top 3 Leadership Strengths:
1.
2.
3.

Key Achievements That Demonstrate Leadership Impact:
-
-

My 90-Day Entry Plan (Key Priorities):
-

By completing this Leadership Profile, you will be fully prepared to step into leadership roles with confidence, clarity, and purpose.

Building Your Leadership Future

A strong leadership foundation is about more than qualifications—it is about purpose, strategy, and vision. By defining who you are as a leader, crafting a compelling resume, conducting in-depth research, and preparing an entry plan, you are positioning yourself not just for a job, but for long-term impact.

Take action. Refine your leadership profile and start applying with intention!

Chapter 4
Cultivating Connections
Relationships, Networks, and Allies

Chapter 4

Cultivating Connections – Relationships, Networks, and Allies

Leadership is Not a Solo Journey

Effective leadership is not just about **what you know**—it's about **who you know, who supports you, and how you navigate professional networks** (Bryk & Schneider, 2002). Research consistently shows that **leaders with strong professional relationships, active engagement in networks, and solid community ties are more successful in advancing their careers and enacting meaningful change** (Fullan, 2014; Coleman & LaRoque, 2020).

For **women and leaders of color**, cultivating **intentional relationships** is particularly crucial. Many marginalized leaders lack the **built-in mentorship and sponsorship** that their White male counterparts often receive (Miller & Garran, 2017). To navigate these barriers, aspiring leaders must be **strategic about building networks, engaging allies, and leveraging affinity groups** that foster leadership development and advocacy (New Leaders, 2022).

This chapter will explore how to:

- Build and sustain professional relationships that support career advancement;
- Leverage networks and affinity groups to access opportunities and mentorship;
- Engage community stakeholders to establish trust and credibility in leadership roles.

By the end of this chapter, you will have **clear strategies and action steps** to strengthen your professional connections and leadership presence.

Building and Sustaining Professional Relationships

Leadership is relational. Whether you are an **aspiring principal, district leader, or superintendent**, your ability to **collaborate, communicate, and connect** with others will **shape your career trajectory** (Bryk & Schneider, 2002).

The Power of Mentorship and Sponsorship

- **Mentors** provide **guidance, feedback, and encouragement** to help you grow as a leader.

- **Sponsors** go a step further—they **advocate for you, connect you with opportunities, and actively support your career advancement** (Ibarra, Carter, & Silva, 2010).

Key Research on Mentorship and Sponsorship:
📖 Ibarra, H., Carter, N., & Silva, C. (2010). WHY MEN STILL GET MORE PROMOTIONS THAN WOMEN. **Harvard Business Review.**

- Found that **women and people of color tend to have mentors rather than sponsors**, limiting their access to high-level opportunities.

- **Sponsorship is critical for advancement** because sponsors use their **influence to recommend protégés for leadership roles.**

📖 Miller, P., & Garran, P. (2017). BIAS AND HIRING IN EDUCATIONAL LEADERSHIP: A REVIEW. **Journal of School Leadership.**

- Identifies how **informal networks influence hiring decisions**, often favoring White male candidates.

- Suggests that **leaders from underrepresented backgrounds need intentional mentorship and visibility strategies** to counteract biases.

📖 New Leaders (2022). THE SHOULDER TAP: EDUCATORS OF COLOR ON THE LEADERSHIP REPRESENTATION GAP.

- Highlights that **aspiring leaders of color are less likely to receive informal career encouragement** compared to White colleagues.

- Recommends **structured mentorship programs** to increase **representation in leadership pipelines.**

Strategies for Building Professional Relationships:

- **Seek out both mentors and sponsors.** Identify experienced leaders who can **provide guidance** (mentor) and **actively advocate for your advancement** (sponsor).

- **Be visible in leadership spaces.** Attend **conferences, district meetings, and leadership workshops** where key decision-makers are present.

- **Maintain regular check-ins. Schedule quarterly meetings** with mentors/sponsors to discuss career progress and opportunities.

📌 Action Step:
Make a list of 3-5 **potential mentors or sponsors in your field** and reach out for an **informational meeting or virtual coffee chat** to start building these relationships.

Leveraging Networks and Affinity Groups

Your **network is one of the most valuable assets** in your leadership journey. Professional associations and **affinity groups** provide:
✓ Mentorship and peer support
✓ Leadership development opportunities
✓ Access to job postings and career advancement programs

The Role of Affinity Groups in Leadership Development

For **leaders from underrepresented backgrounds, affinity groups provide a vital space for professional growth and advocacy** (Jean-Marie, Normore, & Brooks, 2009).

Key Research on Affinity Groups and Networking:

📖 Jean-Marie, G., Normore, A. H., & Brooks, J. S. (2009). LEADERSHIP FOR SOCIAL JUSTICE: PREPARING 21ST CENTURY SCHOOL LEADERS.

- Argues that **networking and affinity groups play a crucial role in diversifying educational leadership.**
- Calls for **intentional development programs that support women and leaders of color** in career advancement.

📖 Wallace Foundation (2021). HOW PRINCIPALS AFFECT STUDENTS AND SCHOOLS: A SYSTEMATIC SYNTHESIS OF TWO DECADES OF RESEARCH.

- Recommends **creating formal principal mentorship networks** to support **new and aspiring leaders.**

📖 AASA (2023). THE TIME IS NOW: A PLAYBOOK FOR WOMEN IN EDUCATIONAL LEADERSHIP.

- Provides **a roadmap for women leaders**, emphasizing **networking, sponsorship, and strategic visibility.**

Top Networks and Affinity Groups for Educational Leaders:

- **Association of Latino Administrators and Superintendents (ALAS)** – Focuses on **Latino leadership in education.**
- **National Alliance of Black School Educators (NABSE)** – Supports **Black educators in advancing to leadership positions.**
- **AASA Women in Leadership Initiative** – Aims to **increase female representation in the superintendency.**
- **NAESP & NASSP Leadership Networks** – Provide **mentorship programs and leadership development for principals.**

📌 Action Step:
Join at least one **leadership network or affinity group** that aligns with your career goals. **Engage actively** by attending events and contributing to discussions.

Engaging Community Stakeholders for Leadership Success

Beyond professional networks, **engaging with community stakeholders is essential for effective leadership** (Bryk, Sebring, Allensworth, Luppescu, & Easton, 2010). Successful school leaders build strong relationships with **parents, teachers, and local organizations** to ensure **equity-driven, community-centered decision-making** (Ishimaru, 2019).

The Role of Community Engagement in Educational Leadership

- **Leaders who actively engage with families and community members** foster **greater trust, collaboration, and student success** (Ishimaru, 2019).

- **Strong school-community partnerships** contribute to **higher academic achievement, increased parent involvement, and positive school culture** (Bryk et al., 2010).

Key Research on Community Engagement in School Leadership:

📖 Bryk, A. S., Sebring, P. B., Allensworth, E., Luppescu, S., & Easton, J. Q. (2010). ORGANIZING SCHOOLS FOR IMPROVEMENT: LESSONS FROM CHICAGO.

- Found that **schools with strong community partnerships saw significant improvements in student achievement and school culture.**

📖 Ishimaru, A. M. (2019). JUST SCHOOLS: BUILDING EQUITABLE COLLABORATIONS WITH FAMILIES AND COMMUNITIES.

- Argues that **school leaders must shift from "community outreach" to authentic, collaborative partnerships** that **empower families as co-leaders.**

Strategies for Engaging Community Stakeholders:

- **Host town halls and listening sessions.** Create opportunities for parents and community members to share concerns and ideas.

- **Partner with local organizations.** Collaborate with **nonprofits, businesses, and faith-based groups** to support school initiatives.

- **Incorporate family engagement in leadership decisions.** Ensure **parents and students** have a **seat at the table** when discussing policies and school improvements.

📌 **Action Step:**
Identify a **key community stakeholder (parent group, local business, or nonprofit) and schedule a meeting** to discuss potential partnerships.

Building a Leadership Ecosystem

Leadership is **not a solitary pursuit**—it thrives through **relationships, networks, and community engagement**. By **cultivating mentorship and sponsorship, joining professional networks, and building strong stakeholder relationships**, you create **a powerful leadership ecosystem** that supports your **growth, impact, and career advancement**.

Take action today by **identifying a mentor, joining a leadership network, or engaging with your community stakeholders**. Your network **is your leadership currency—invest in it wisely!**

Chapter 5
Weathering the Storms
Navigating Challenges with Grace

Chapter 5

Weathering the Storms – Navigating Challenges with Grace

The Resilient Leader

Leadership is not just about vision and strategy—it is about **resilience in the face of adversity**. Every school leader will encounter **crises, conflicts, and moments of uncertainty**, but what distinguishes **great leaders** from the rest is their **ability to navigate challenges with composure, emotional intelligence, and strategic thinking** (Heifetz, Grashow, & Linsky, 2009).

For **women and leaders of color**, leadership often comes with **additional hurdles**, including **heightened scrutiny, systemic barriers, and the need to constantly balance advocacy with diplomacy** (Jean-Marie, Normore, & Brooks, 2009). Knowing **how to manage crises, engage in difficult conversations, and advocate for change while maintaining credibility** is critical for sustaining **a long and impactful leadership career**.

This chapter explores how to:
Lead through adversity and crisis with confidence and clarity
Manage conflict and engage in difficult conversations effectively
Balance advocacy with diplomacy to enact meaningful change without political fallout

By the end of this chapter, you will have **practical strategies and tools** to help you navigate **leadership challenges with resilience, strategic thinking, and emotional intelligence**.

Leading Through Adversity and Crisis

Crisis is inevitable in leadership. Whether dealing with **a school safety issue, a budget crisis, a public relations challenge, or a global pandemic**, leaders must respond **decisively and effectively** (Fullan, 2014; Goleman, 1998).

Key Leadership Strategies for Crisis Management

1. Stay Calm and Centered

- Research on **emotional intelligence** shows that **leaders who remain calm under pressure inspire confidence and trust** (Goleman, 1998).
- **Tip: Pause before reacting**—take a deep breath, assess the situation, and respond strategically rather than emotionally.

2. Communicate Clearly and Transparently

- During a crisis, **clear and honest communication is essential** (Coombs, 2014).
- **Tip:** Provide **timely updates** and control the narrative—if leaders don't communicate, misinformation will.

3. **Engage Key Stakeholders Early**

- **Collaboration builds trust**—engage teachers, parents, and community members **before making major decisions**(Bryk & Schneider, 2002).
- **Tip: Create a crisis response team** in advance so roles and responsibilities are clear when challenges arise.

Key Research on Leading Through Crisis:
📖 Fullan, M. (2014). LEADING IN A CULTURE OF CHANGE.

- Highlights **how adaptive leadership** is necessary in **times of uncertainty** and how **leaders must model resilience**.

📖 Goleman, D. (1998). WORKING WITH EMOTIONAL INTELLIGENCE.

- Research demonstrates that **leaders with high emotional intelligence** are more effective in handling **crises and high-pressure situations**.

📖 Coombs, W. T. (2014). ONGOING CRISIS COMMUNICATION: PLANNING, MANAGING, AND RESPONDING.

- Provides a **framework for strategic crisis communication** in educational and organizational settings.

📌 Action Step:
Identify a recent crisis in your district or school. How was it handled? What lessons can you learn from the response to apply to your own leadership approach?

Managing Conflict and Difficult Conversations

Conflict is **unavoidable in leadership**, whether it involves **disagreements with staff, policy disputes, or tensions with parents and community members** (Ury, 1991). Effective leaders know how to navigate conflict productively rather than avoiding or escalating it (Stone, Patton, & Heen, 2010).

Best Practices for Managing Conflict as a School Leader

1. Listen to Understand, Not to Respond

- Research shows that **active listening** is the most effective way to de-escalate conflict (Ury, 1991).
- **Tip:** Use **reflective listening**—repeat back what you hear to **demonstrate understanding before responding**.

2. Use "I" Statements and Keep Conversations Solution-Oriented

- Frame discussions in a way that **avoids blame** and **focuses on solutions** (Stone et al., 2010).
- **Tip:** Instead of saying "YOU'RE NOT SUPPORTING TEACHERS," try "I WANT TO ENSURE WE ARE ALIGNED IN SUPPORTING OUR TEACHERS–HOW CAN WE COLLABORATE MORE EFFECTIVELY?"

3. Know When to Escalate and When to Mediate

- Not all conflicts can be resolved internally—**some require mediation or intervention from district officials**(Kirtman, 2013).
- **Tip:** If a situation is escalating, **involve a neutral third party** to facilitate a resolution.

Key Research on Conflict Management in Leadership:
📖 Ury, W. (1991). GETTING PAST NO: NEGOTIATING IN DIFFICULT SITUATIONS.

- Discusses strategies for **turning conflict into cooperation** using **negotiation and active listening techniques**.

📖 Stone, D., Patton, B., & Heen, S. (2010). DIFFICULT CONVERSATIONS: HOW TO DISCUSS WHAT MATTERS MOST.

- Provides **a framework for handling emotionally charged conversations** in leadership.

📖 Kirtman, L. (2013). LEADERSHIP AND TEAMS: THE MISSING PIECE OF THE EDUCATIONAL REFORM PUZZLE.

- Examines how **leaders can foster collaboration and manage resistance to change**.

📌 Action Step:
Practice the "3-Step Conflict Resolution Model":
1. **Acknowledge the concern** ("I HEAR THAT THIS IS FRUSTRATING FOR YOU.")
2. **Find common ground** ("WE BOTH WANT WHAT'S BEST FOR OUR STUDENTS.")
3. **Propose a next step** ("LET'S EXPLORE SOLUTIONS TOGETHER.")

Balancing Advocacy with Diplomacy

Leaders must **advocate for equity and systemic change**, but they must also **navigate political realities** and maintain **credibility among diverse stakeholders** (Jean-Marie et al., 2009). Effective advocacy requires balancing bold **leadership with strategic diplomacy.**

How to Advocate for Change Without Political Backlash

1. **Know When to Push and When to Pause**

    - **Strategic patience** can be as effective as **immediate action** (Heifetz & Linsky, 2002).

    - **Tip:** Read the **organizational climate** before pushing an agenda—**timing matters.**

2. **Build Coalitions and Gather Allies**

    - Change doesn't happen alone—**align yourself with other influential leaders and stakeholders** (Kouzes & Posner, 2017).

    - **Tip:** Identify **key allies who share your vision** and work together to build momentum.

3. **Frame the Message for Maximum Impact**

    - **How you communicate matters as much as what you communicate** (Eagly & Carli, 2007).

    - **Tip:** Use **data, storytelling, and stakeholder concerns** to shape a compelling argument for change.

Key Research on Advocacy and Diplomacy in Leadership:

📖 Jean-Marie, G., Normore, A. H., & Brooks, J. S. (2009). LEADERSHIP FOR SOCIAL JUSTICE: PREPARING 21ST CENTURY SCHOOL LEADERS.

- Discusses **how marginalized leaders must navigate advocacy in politically charged environments.**

📖 Heifetz, R. A., & Linsky, M. (2002). LEADERSHIP ON THE LINE: STAYING ALIVE THROUGH THE DANGERS OF LEADING.

- Offers **strategies for leading difficult change efforts without alienating key stakeholders.**

📖 Eagly, A. H., & Carli, L. L. (2007). THROUGH THE LABYRINTH: THE TRUTH ABOUT HOW WOMEN BECOME LEADERS.

- Analyzes how **women leaders must balance assertiveness with diplomacy to advance.**

📌 **Action Step:**
Identify a policy or initiative you want to advocate for in your district. Develop a **strategic advocacy plan**, including key **stakeholders, messaging, and timing.**

Leadership in the Eye of the Storm

Navigating challenges **with grace, resilience, and strategic thinking** is essential for **long-term success in leadership.** By **leading with composure, engaging in conflict productively, and advocating strategically,** you will establish yourself as a **credible, effective, and equity-driven leader.**

Next Step: Reflect on a **current or past leadership challenge** you've faced. What **lessons can you apply** to **future** leadership situations.

"Effective leadership succession is not about planting a single flower; it's about cultivating a field of dandelions—adaptable, resilient, and prepared to rise wherever they land."

-Dr. LeAnne Salazar Montoya

Chapter 6

Blooming in Leadership

Leading with Purpose and Impact

Chapter 6

Blooming in Leadership – Leading with Purpose and Impact

Growing into a Transformational Leader

Leadership is not just about managing systems—it is about **inspiring, empowering, and driving change**. **Transformational leaders cultivate strong teams, advocate for equity, and create environments where students, teachers, and communities thrive** (Bass & Riggio, 2006).

For **women and leaders of color**, leading with purpose often means **navigating resistance, advocating for change, and breaking barriers** that have historically limited access to leadership positions (Eagly & Carli, 2007). True leadership requires **vision, resilience, and the ability to inspire others to work toward a common goal** (Kouzes & Posner, 2017).

This chapter explores how to:
Implement transformational leadership strategies that create lasting impact
Lead for equity by putting advocacy into action
Strengthen team culture and morale to build high-performing, motivated teams

By the end of this chapter, you will have **research-backed strategies** and **practical tools** to lead with authenticity, inspire meaningful change, and cultivate an environment of excellence.

Transformational Leadership Strategies

Transformational leadership is cantered on **inspiring and empowering others to achieve a shared vision** (Bass, 1990). Rather than maintaining the status quo, transformational leaders **challenge existing norms, encourage innovation, and develop future leaders** (Fullan, 2014).

Four Pillars of Transformational Leadership (Bass & Riggio, 2006)

1. **Inspirational Motivation** – Leaders **create a compelling vision** and **rally their teams toward a common goal**.
2. **Intellectual Stimulation** – They encourage creativity, critical thinking, and problem-solving.
3. **Individualized Consideration** – They **support and develop each team member**, ensuring **personal and professional growth**.
4. **Idealized Influence (Modeling the Way)** – They **lead by example**, earning respect and trust through **integrity, authenticity, and ethical decision-making**.

Key Research on Transformational Leadership:
📖 Bass, B. M. (1990). FROM TRANSACTIONAL TO TRANSFORMATIONAL LEADERSHIP: LEARNING TO SHARE THE VISION.

- **Introduced the transformational leadership model** and showed how leaders can **drive organizational change through vision and motivation**.

📖 **Kouzes, J. M., & Posner, B. Z. (2017).** THE LEADERSHIP CHALLENGE: HOW TO MAKE EXTRAORDINARY THINGS HAPPEN IN ORGANIZATIONS.

- Identifies five essential leadership practices: **model the way, inspire a shared vision, challenge the process, enable others to act, and encourage the heart.**

📖 **Fullan, M. (2014).** LEADING IN A CULTURE OF CHANGE.

- Highlights how transformational leaders must **navigate resistance and guide schools through sustainable change.**

Strategies for Implementing Transformational Leadership:

- **Develop a leadership vision statement** that aligns with **equity, student success, and school improvement.**
- **Encourage leadership at all levels**—empower teachers and staff to take initiative.
- **Foster a growth mindset**—create a culture where learning, risk-taking, and innovation are encouraged.

📌 Action Step:
Write your personal leadership vision statement. Define what kind of leader you are and how you inspire change.

Leading for Equity: Advocacy in Action

Equity leadership is about **identifying and addressing systemic barriers to ensure all students, regardless of background, have access to high-quality education** (Khalifa, Gooden, & Davis, 2016). Advocacy is not just a belief—it is an action.

Key Components of Equity-Centered Leadership

1. **Equity Audits and Data-Driven Decision Making**

- Leaders must **examine disparities in student outcomes** (graduation rates, disciplinary actions, academic performance).
- **Tip:** Use **disaggregated data** to **identify inequities and drive policy changes.**

2. **Culturally Responsive Leadership**

- Schools should **reflect the diverse identities of their students** (Ladson-Billings, 1995).
- **Tip: Implement professional development on cultural competence** for staff.

3. **Policy and Systemic Advocacy**

- **School leaders must advocate for policies** that close opportunity gaps (Ishimaru, 2019).

- **Tip: Engage in state and district-level decision-making** to drive equity initiatives.

Key Research on Leading for Equity:

📖 Khalifa, M., Gooden, M. A., & Davis, J. E. (2016). CULTURALLY RESPONSIVE SCHOOL LEADERSHIP: A SYNTHESIS OF THE LITERATURE.

- Emphasizes **the importance of racial equity, community engagement, and culturally affirming practices.**

📖 Ladson-Billings, G. (1995). TOWARD A THEORY OF CULTURALLY RELEVANT PEDAGOGY.

- Highlights the **role of culturally responsive teaching and leadership in closing achievement gaps.**

📖 Ishimaru, A. M. (2019). JUST SCHOOLS: BUILDING EQUITABLE COLLABORATIONS WITH FAMILIES AND COMMUNITIES.

- Advocates for **inclusive leadership that actively involves families and communities** in decision-making.

Strategies for Leading with Equity:

- **Conduct equity audits** to assess gaps in student achievement and resource allocation.
- **Implement restorative justice practices** instead of punitive discipline models.
- **Advocate for inclusive curriculum changes** that reflect diverse student identities.

📌 Action Step:
Choose an equity issue in your school and draft an advocacy plan outlining the **steps needed to create meaningful change.**

Strengthening Team Culture and Morale

A **strong school culture** fosters **engagement, collaboration, and commitment** among staff and students (Bryk & Schneider, 2002). Leaders who **prioritize morale and team-building create environments where people feel valued and motivated** (Maslach & Leiter, 2016).

How to Strengthen Team Culture as a Leader

1. **Create a Culture of Trust and Psychological Safety**
   - Leaders who foster open communication and trust build stronger, high-performing teams (Edmondson, 2019).
   - **Tip:** Encourage **feedback, active listening, and open-door leadership.**

2. **Recognize and Celebrate Contributions**
   - Recognition **boosts morale and reinforces positive behaviors** (Maslach & Leiter, 2016).
   - **Tip:** Establish **formal and informal ways to acknowledge staff achievements.**

3. **Build Collective Efficacy Among Educators**
   - **Teachers and staff need to feel that their work has purpose and impact** (Goddard, Hoy, & Woolfolk Hoy, 2000).
   - **Tip: Involve staff in decision-making** and provide leadership opportunities.

Key Research on School Culture and Morale:

📖 Bryk, A. S., & Schneider, B. (2002). TRUST IN SCHOOLS: A CORE RESOURCE FOR IMPROVEMENT.
   - Examines **how relational trust among teachers, students, and leaders improves school performance.**

📖 Edmondson, A. C. (2019). THE FEARLESS ORGANIZATION: CREATING PSYCHOLOGICAL SAFETY IN THE WORKPLACE FOR LEARNING, INNOVATION, AND GROWTH.
   - Highlights how **leaders can cultivate safe, inclusive environments where teams thrive.**

📖 Maslach, C., & Leiter, M. P. (2016). BURNOUT: THE COST OF CARING.
   - Explores **how leadership influences employee engagement and burnout.**

Strategies for Boosting Team Morale:
- **Schedule regular team-building activities** to strengthen relationships.
- **Provide professional development that aligns with teachers' growth interests.**
- **Celebrate milestones and small wins** to reinforce motivation.

📌 **Action Step:**
Create a "Culture-Building Plan" with 3 strategies you will implement to **boost team morale and strengthen relationships** in your school.

Leading with Purpose, Creating Lasting Impact

Leadership is about impact, not position. By embracing **transformational leadership, leading for equity, and fostering a strong team culture,** you will **inspire change, uplift communities, and create meaningful progress in education.**

Reflect on **how your leadership approach embodies transformational leadership** and **commit to one actionable step** you will take to **strengthen your impact.**

Chapter 7

Seeing the Future

Mentorship and Legacy Building

Chapter 7

Seeding the Future – Mentorship and Legacy Building

The True Measure of Leadership is Legacy

Great leaders do not just **achieve personal success**—they **create pathways for others** to follow. Leadership is a **continuous cycle of learning, mentoring, and uplifting the next generation** (Collins, 2001). For **women and leaders of color, mentorship and sponsorship are essential tools for dismantling barriers** and ensuring that underrepresented voices **thrive in leadership spaces** (Ibarra, Carter, & Silva, 2010).

True leadership extends beyond **individual achievement**—it is about **seeding the future, building sustainable leadership pipelines, and leaving a lasting impact on education.** This chapter will explore how to:
Pay it forward by mentoring and lifting others as you climb
Create leadership pipelines that support underrepresented educators
Craft a lasting impact that extends beyond your tenure

By the end of this chapter, you will have **strategies to mentor future leaders, develop equity-driven leadership pipelines, and leave a legacy that transforms educational leadership for generations to come.**

Paying It Forward: Lifting Others as You Climb

Leadership should not be **a solitary journey**—it should be **a movement that brings others along.** Research shows that **leaders who actively mentor and develop others create stronger, more inclusive workplaces** (Kram, 1985).

The Power of Sponsorship and Mentorship in Leadership

Mentorship – A mentor **guides, advises, and supports** emerging leaders.
Sponsorship – A sponsor **advocates, connects, and actively champions** someone for leadership roles (Ibarra et al., 2010).

Key Research on Mentorship in Leadership Development:
📖 Ibarra, H., Carter, N. M., & Silva, C. (2010). WHY MEN STILL GET MORE PROMOTIONS THAN WOMEN. **Harvard Business Review.**

- Found that **women and leaders of color are often over-mentored but under-sponsored,** meaning they receive advice but lack active advocates pushing them forward.

📖 Kram, K. E. (1985). MENTORING AT WORK: DEVELOPMENTAL RELATIONSHIPS IN ORGANIZATIONAL LIFE.

- A foundational study that **explores how mentorship relationships influence career development.**

📖 Jean-Marie, G., Normore, A. H., & Brooks, J. S. (2009). LEADERSHIP FOR SOCIAL JUSTICE: PREPARING 21ST CENTURY SCHOOL LEADERS.

- Discusses how **mentorship and networking help underrepresented leaders navigate systemic challenges**.

Strategies for Mentoring and Sponsoring Emerging Leaders:
✔ **Be intentional about mentorship**—reach out to rising educators and offer guidance.
✔ **Sponsor emerging leaders**—advocate for mentees in hiring discussions and leadership opportunities.
✔ **Create mentorship circles**—connect multiple leaders to foster **collective growth and support**.

📌 **Action Step:**
Identify an emerging leader in your network. Offer mentorship or sponsorship by sharing insights, connecting them to opportunities, or advocating for their advancement.

Creating Sustainable Leadership Pipelines for Underrepresented Leaders

For **systemic change to occur, we must intentionally build leadership pipelines that uplift marginalized educators**(Fuller & Young, 2022). The lack of diversity in educational leadership is **not a talent issue—it is a pipeline issue**(Bailes & Guthery, 2020).

Addressing the Gaps in Leadership Pipelines

1️. **Barriers to Leadership for Women and Leaders of Color**

- **Lack of mentorship and sponsorship** (New Leaders, 2022)
- **Bias in hiring and promotions** (Bailes & Guthery, 2020)
- **Limited access to high-visibility leadership roles** (Eagly & Carli, 2007)

2️. **The Role of Leadership Development Programs**

- Programs such as **AASA's Women in Leadership Initiative**, **NAESP's Principals of Color Network**, and **ALAS' Aspiring Latino Superintendents Program** help bridge gaps in leadership representation.

Key Research on Leadership Pipelines:
📖 Fuller, E. J., & Young, M. D. (2022). CHALLENGES AND OPPORTUNITIES IN DIVERSIFYING THE LEADERSHIP PIPELINE. **Leadership and Policy in Schools.**

- Examines **where educators of color exit the leadership pipeline** and identifies strategies to **increase leadership diversity**.

📖 Bailes, L. P., & Guthery, S. (2020). HELD DOWN AND HELD BACK: SYSTEMATICALLY DELAYED PRINCIPAL PROMOTIONS BY RACE AND GENDER. **AERA Open, 6(2).**

- Provides **quantitative evidence of systemic biases** in **promotions for women and leaders of color**.

📖 New Leaders (2022). THE SHOULDER TAP: EDUCATORS OF COLOR ON THE LEADERSHIP REPRESENTATION GAP.

- Found that **personalized mentorship and intentional recruitment** significantly improve leadership opportunities for marginalized educators.

Strategies for Strengthening Leadership Pipelines:
✔ **Establish leadership training cohorts** for aspiring leaders from underrepresented backgrounds.
✔ Work with district officials to create transparent hiring and promotion pathways.
✔ Advocate for systemic changes, including diverse hiring committees and equitable access to leadership programs.

📌 **Action Step:**
Identify a leadership pipeline initiative in your district. Explore ways to **participate, support, or advocate for its expansion.**

Crafting a Lasting Impact in Education

True leadership is about **planting seeds that will grow long after you are gone.** Legacy-building means **creating systems, programs, and cultures that sustain equity, growth, and excellence** (Collins, 2001).

Three Pillars of Leadership Legacy

1. **Impact on People** – Have you **mentored and uplifted others?**
2. **Impact on Systems** – Have you **created policies and structures that will outlast your tenure?**
3. **Impact on Culture** – Have you **shifted mindsets and institutional norms** toward equity and inclusivity?

Key Research on Leadership Legacy:
📖 Collins, J. (2001). GOOD TO GREAT: WHY SOME COMPANIES MAKE THE LEAP… AND OTHERS DON'T.

- Argues that **the best leaders focus on sustainability and long-term impact,** rather than short-term success.

📖 Kouzes, J. M., & Posner, B. Z. (2017). THE LEADERSHIP CHALLENGE.

- Examines **how the most successful leaders cultivate future leadership and create lasting influence.**

📖 Edmondson, A. C. (2019). THE FEARLESS ORGANIZATION: CREATING PSYCHOLOGICAL SAFETY IN THE WORKPLACE.

- Discusses how **leaders who build inclusive cultures create workplaces where innovation and leadership flourish.**

Strategies for Crafting a Leadership Legacy:
✔ **Develop mentorship programs** within your school or district.
✔ Institutionalize equity-driven leadership practices.
✔ Create and document best practices that future leaders can build upon.

📌 Action Step:
Write a Leadership Legacy Statement:

- What do you want to be remembered for as a leader?

- How will your leadership impact the next generation?

- What structures or systems will you leave behind that sustain growth and equity?

The Future of Leadership is in Your Hands

Leadership is not about **personal titles or recognition**—it is about **creating opportunities for others, dismantling barriers, and leaving a lasting impact.**

As you continue your leadership journey:
🌱 **Mentor and sponsor emerging leaders**—pay it forward.
🌱 **Advocate for leadership pipelines that uplift underrepresented voices.**
🌱 **Leave behind a legacy that strengthens education for future generations.**

Reflect on your **leadership impact**—who have you **mentored, sponsored, or uplifted**? What more can you **do to seed the future of leadership?**

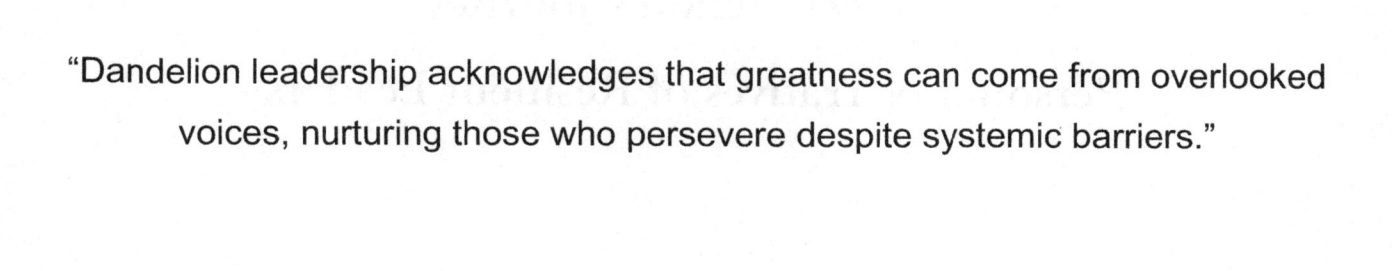

"Dandelion leadership acknowledges that greatness can come from overlooked voices, nurturing those who persevere despite systemic barriers."

Chapter 8

The Dandelion's Journey

Personal Narratives of Resilient Leaders

Chapter 8

The Dandelion's Journey – Personal Narratives of Resilient Leaders

The Power of Storytelling in Leadership

Resilience is not just a **trait**—it is a **journey**. Every leader's path is shaped by **challenges, triumphs, and lessons learned** along the way. For **women, leaders of color, and other marginalized educators**, the road to leadership often requires **perseverance, self-advocacy, and an unwavering belief in the power of education to create change** (Jean-Marie, Normore, & Brooks, 2009).

In this chapter, we will explore:
Stories from diverse school leaders who have navigated adversity and thrived
Lessons learned and advice for aspiring leaders
Reflections on identity, perseverance, and empowerment

By sharing these personal narratives, we honour **the resilience of marginalized leaders** and provide **aspiring educators with insights and inspiration** as they step into leadership roles.

Stories from Diverse, Marginalized School Leaders

Throughout history, **educational leadership has been shaped by individuals who defied the odds and paved the way for others**. These stories reflect the **dandelion's journey**—pushing through adversity, taking root in challenging conditions, and spreading seeds of change.

Disclaimer: The names of these leaders have been shared through pseudonyms to protect the identity of the leaders who have made themselves vulnerable and shared their narratives. Practicing leaders have everything to lose when they make themselves vulnerable and for the purpose of this manual their names are protected.

A Superintendent's Story: Breaking Barriers as a Latina Leader

📖 DR. MARIA GONZALEZ, SUPERINTENDENT OF A LARGE URBAN DISTRICT, REFLECTS ON HER JOURNEY:

"I WAS OFTEN THE ONLY LATINA IN LEADERSHIP MEETINGS. I HAD TO FIGHT FOR A SEAT AT THE TABLE, NOT JUST FOR MYSELF, BUT FOR THE STUDENTS WHO NEEDED REPRESENTATION. EARLY IN MY CAREER, I WAS TOLD I WAS 'TOO PASSIONATE' ABOUT EQUITY, AS IF THAT WAS A FLAW. BUT I REFUSED TO SHRINK MYSELF. I FOUND ALLIES, MENTORS, AND EVENTUALLY BECAME A SPONSOR FOR OTHER WOMEN OF COLOR IN LEADERSHIP."

💡 Lesson Learned:

- **Advocate boldly**—don't wait for permission to lead.
- **Representation matters**—seeing a Latina superintendent inspires the next generation.

Research Connection:
📖 Méndez-Morse, S. (2004). LATINA SCHOOL LEADERS: CHALLENGES AND STRENGTHS.

- Examines how **Latina leaders navigate cultural, gender, and systemic barriers** in educational leadership.

An Assistant Principal's Story: Leading as a Black Male Educator

📖 MR. JAMAL CARTER, AN ASSISTANT PRINCIPAL AT A PREDOMINANTLY WHITE SCHOOL, SHARES:

"I WAS ALWAYS EXPECTED TO HANDLE DISCIPLINE, NOT CURRICULUM. THERE'S AN ASSUMPTION THAT BLACK MALE EDUCATORS BELONG IN SECURITY OR BEHAVIOR MANAGEMENT. I HAD TO PUSH BACK AND ASSERT THAT I WAS JUST AS QUALIFIED TO LEAD INSTRUCTIONAL PRACTICES. I SOUGHT MENTORS, TOOK ON LEADERSHIP ROLES THAT ALIGNED WITH MY EXPERTISE, AND EVENTUALLY CHANGED THE PERCEPTION OF WHAT A BLACK MALE LEADER COULD BE."

💡 Lesson Learned:

- **Challenge stereotypes**—you define your leadership path.
- **Seek leadership beyond what is expected of you**—expand into academic and administrative roles.

Research Connection:
📖 Brown, A. L. (2012). ON HUMAN KINDS AND ROLE MODELS: A CRITICAL DISCUSSION ABOUT THE AFRICAN AMERICAN MALE TEACHER.

- Discusses **racial stereotypes in education** and the **importance of Black male role models in leadership**.

A Principal's Story: Overcoming Imposter Syndrome as a First-Generation Leader

📖 DR. AISHA PATEL, A PRINCIPAL FROM A LOW-INCOME IMMIGRANT BACKGROUND, REFLECTS:

"WHEN I STEPPED INTO MY FIRST LEADERSHIP ROLE, I FELT LIKE A FRAUD. I CONSTANTLY QUESTIONED IF I WAS GOOD ENOUGH. IT TOOK YEARS OF SELF-REFLECTION AND MENTORSHIP TO REALIZE THAT I BELONGED. NOW, I MENTOR FIRST-GENERATION EDUCATORS, REMINDING THEM THAT THEIR UNIQUE EXPERIENCES ARE AN ASSET, NOT A LIMITATION."

Lesson Learned:

- **Imposter syndrome is common**—acknowledge it but don't let it define you.
- Your **lived experience makes you a more empathetic and effective leader**.

Research Connection:
📖 Clance, P. R., & Imes, S. A. (1978). THE IMPOSTER PHENOMENON IN HIGH ACHIEVING WOMEN: DYNAMICS AND THERAPEUTIC INTERVENTION.

- Introduced the concept of **imposter syndrome**, showing how **women and underrepresented groups struggle with self-doubt despite their qualifications**.

Lessons Learned and Advice for Aspiring Leaders

📌 **Insights from Marginalized School Leaders:**

✓ **You Belong in Leadership**

- "DON'T INTERNALIZE THE DOUBTS OTHERS PROJECT ONTO YOU. IF YOU'RE IN THE ROOM, YOU BELONG THERE."

✓ **Find Your Circle of Support**

- "YOU NEED MENTORS, SPONSORS, AND PEERS WHO UPLIFT YOU. BUILD YOUR SUPPORT SYSTEM."

✓ **Lead with Authenticity**

- "YOU DON'T HAVE TO CHANGE WHO YOU ARE TO FIT INTO LEADERSHIP. THE BEST LEADERS BRING THEIR FULL SELVES TO THE ROLE."

✓ **Pay It Forward**

- "AS YOU RISE, LIFT OTHERS. MAKE MENTORSHIP A PRIORITY."

Key Research on Leadership Development for Underrepresented Leaders:

📖 Eagly, A. H., & Carli, L. L. (2007). THROUGH THE LABYRINTH: THE TRUTH ABOUT HOW WOMEN BECOME LEADERS.

- Examines how **women navigate non-linear leadership paths** and **overcome systemic barriers**.

📖 Jean-Marie, G. (2008). LEADERSHIP FOR SOCIAL JUSTICE: PREPARING 21ST CENTURY SCHOOL LEADERS.

- Explores **how leaders of color challenge inequities and advocate for systemic change.**

Reflections on Perseverance, Identity, and Empowerment

Leadership requires **resilience, courage, and a deep sense of purpose.** Every challenge faced is an opportunity for **growth, advocacy, and change.**

🌱 **Reflections from School Leaders:**

- "RESILIENCE MEANS STANDING FIRM IN YOUR VALUES, EVEN WHEN SYSTEMS PUSH BACK."
- "YOUR IDENTITY IS YOUR STRENGTH—EMBRACE IT, DON'T DILUTE IT."
- "EMPOWER OTHERS ALONG THE WAY—TRUE LEADERSHIP IS COLLECTIVE, NOT INDIVIDUAL."

Key Research on Identity and Leadership:
📖 Khalifa, M. (2018). CULTURALLY RESPONSIVE SCHOOL LEADERSHIP.

- Highlights how **leaders of color navigate identity, bias, and advocacy** in leadership roles.

📖 hooks, b. (1994). TEACHING TO TRANSGRESS: EDUCATION AS THE PRACTICE OF FREEDOM.

- Argues that **education is a tool for empowerment** and **leaders must center justice and inclusivity.**

Your Story is Still Being Written

The journey of leadership is ongoing. **Each leader's path is unique, yet connected by shared struggles, resilience, and triumphs.** The dandelion's journey—pushing through concrete, adapting, growing in unexpected places—reflects the **strength of marginalized leaders who rise despite the odds.**

Reflect on **your own leadership journey**—what lessons have shaped you? How will you **use your experiences to inspire and uplift others?** Your story is powerful—**keep writing it, keep leading, and keep planting seeds of change.**

"Leaders of color, akin to dandelions, carry seeds of potential that, when intentionally cultivated, reshape the landscape of educational leadership."

-Dr. LeAnne Salazar Montoya

Chapter 9
Blueprint for Breaking Barriers in Educational Leadership

Chapter 9

Blueprint for Breaking Barriers in Educational Leadership

While understanding the systemic challenges of educational leadership is crucial, equipping oneself with actionable strategies is equally essential. Many aspiring leaders from marginalized backgrounds face implicit biases, structural barriers, and limited access to mentorship and sponsorship (Bailes & Guthery, 2020; Jean-Marie, Normore, & Brooks, 2009). However, strategic preparation, intentional networking, and proactive career positioning can help overcome these obstacles and create new pathways to leadership.

This section provides a step-by-step practical blueprint to help marginalized leaders navigate, rise, and thrive in educational leadership roles. Each step includes targeted actions to address bias, build leadership capital, and proactively shape a leadership trajectory that leads to meaningful and lasting impact.

Step 1: Define Your Leadership Identity and Philosophy

A well-defined **leadership philosophy** helps you articulate **who you are as a leader, what you stand for, and how you will make a difference.** Leaders who **clearly define their values, mission, and goals** are more likely to **navigate adversity with confidence** and **stand out in hiring processes** (Grogan & Shakeshaft, 2011).

Actionable Steps:
✓ **Craft a Leadership Vision Statement** – Write a **1-2 sentence statement** summarizing **your leadership philosophy** and **equity-driven impact goals.**
✓ **Identify Your Strengths & Growth Areas** – Conduct a **self-audit** using **leadership competency frameworks** (e.g., Wallace Foundation Principal Standards).
✓ **Develop an Authentic Leadership Brand** – Ensure that **your resume, LinkedIn, and professional presence** reflect your leadership philosophy.

💡 Example Leadership Vision Statement:
"AS A CULTURALLY RESPONSIVE LEADER, I AM COMMITTED TO BUILDING INCLUSIVE SCHOOL COMMUNITIES WHERE ALL STUDENTS, REGARDLESS OF BACKGROUND, THRIVE. MY MISSION IS TO CREATE EQUITABLE LEARNING ENVIRONMENTS, ADVOCATE FOR UNDERREPRESENTED STUDENTS, AND MENTOR EMERGING LEADERS TO ENSURE SUSTAINABLE, SYSTEMIC CHANGE."

Actionable Strategies:
Write Your Leadership Philosophy Statement

- Clearly define **who you are as a leader**, your **core values**, and your **vision for educational leadership**.
- Use guiding prompts:
    - What drives you to pursue leadership?
    - How do you advocate for equity and student success?
    - What makes you uniquely qualified to lead in today's schools?
- Example Framework:
    - **Mission:** (Your purpose in leadership)
    - **Vision:** (What you hope to achieve for your students and staff)
    - **Values:** (What principles guide your decision-making?)

Develop a 3-Word Leadership Brand

Pick three defining words that encapsulate your leadership style (e.g., **Empathetic – Equity-Focused – Transformational**).

Identify Leadership Role Models

Study **trailblazing leaders** who have paved the way in educational leadership.

Learn from **mentorship networks** (AASA's Women in Leadership, ALAS for Latino Administrators, NABSE for Black School Educators).

Create an Elevator Pitch for Your Leadership

Be able to **articulate who you are in 30 seconds**. Example:
"I am an equity-driven educational leader dedicated to transforming school culture through culturally responsive leadership. My mission is to ensure every student, regardless of background, receives high-quality education by creating an inclusive learning environment."

Step 2: Build a Modern, Competitive Resume

Why It Matters:
Relationships open doors that qualifications alone cannot. **Sponsors and mentors** provide **career opportunities, guidance, and advocacy**—especially for leaders who may be overlooked due to bias (Ibarra, Carter, & Silva, 2010).

Actionable Steps:
✓ **Identify a Mentor & Sponsor** – Seek out **experienced leaders** who align with **your values** and can **provide career guidance and opportunities.**
✓ **Join Professional Organizations** – Engage with **ALAS, NABSE, NAESP, AASA, and Women Leading Ed** to build **meaningful connections and access leadership opportunities.**
✓ **Be Visible in Leadership Circles** – Attend **conferences, present research, and actively contribute to discussions** in leadership spaces.

Pro Tip: Sponsors are **not just mentors**—they actively **advocate for your promotion** in leadership hiring conversations.

Actionable Strategies:
Use the 5-Second Rule

- Hiring managers only glance at resumes for **5–10 seconds** before making a decision.
- Ensure your **top third** has a compelling **leadership summary and key accomplishments.**

Highlight Measurable Leadership Impact

- Avoid generic statements like *"Improved school culture."*
- Use **data-driven results**:
  - "Increased graduation rates from 78% to 92% within three years through targeted equity initiatives."
  - "Led curriculum redesign that resulted in a 25% improvement in standardized test scores."

Use a Two-Column Format for Clarity

- **Left side:** Job Titles, Schools/Districts, Dates
- **Right side:** Key Achievements

Tailor Your Resume for Each Job
- Mirror **language from job descriptions** to pass applicant tracking systems (ATS).
- Include **equity-focused achievements** (e.g., "Implemented culturally responsive pedagogy that increased student engagement by 40%").

Have a Leadership Portfolio Ready
- Collect **letters of recommendation, media coverage, testimonials, and professional development certifications** to supplement applications.

Step 3: Research Where You Apply and Develop an Entry Plan

Hiring processes in education **often favor candidates who demonstrate clear, measurable impact** (Bailes & Guthery, 2020). A modern leadership resume should **go beyond job descriptions** and **showcase achievements using quantifiable outcomes.**

Actionable Steps:
✓ **Highlight Leadership Achievements** – Use **data-driven impact statements** (e.g., "Implemented an intervention program that increased reading proficiency by 22% in two years").
✓ **Tailor Each Resume** – Align your **resume and cover letter with the leadership priorities of the school/district** you're applying to.
✓ **Include Leadership Development** – Showcase **certifications, professional learning, and district-wide initiatives** you have led.

Before & After Resume Example:

✗ ASSISTANT PRINCIPAL, ABC MIDDLE SCHOOL (2018-PRESENT)
- Oversees student discipline and teacher evaluations.
- Implements curriculum and supports instruction.

✓ ASSISTANT PRINCIPAL, ABC MIDDLE SCHOOL (2018-PRESENT)
- **Reduced discipline referrals by 30%** by implementing **restorative justice practices**.
- **Increased ELL reading proficiency by 18%** through targeted instructional coaching.
- **Mentored 15 emerging leaders**, with 7 promoted to administrative roles.

Actionable Strategies:
✓ **Understand the School/District Landscape**
- Research **student demographics, test scores, community priorities, and equity initiatives**.

- Use **EdTrust, NCES, and district data reports** to understand funding and achievement gaps.

✓ **Identify Key Decision-Makers**

- Study the **current superintendent's leadership style** and **board priorities.**
- Network at **statewide education conferences** where hiring officials scout talent.

✓ **Align Your Skills with the District's Needs**

- Position yourself as **the solution** to challenges identified in strategic plans.
- Example: If a district struggles with teacher retention, highlight **how your leadership has improved staff satisfaction and retention rates.**

✓ **Prepare Your First 90-Day Entry Plan**

- At the interview stage, **present a structured, research-backed plan** outlining:
  1. **Listening & Learning Phase (30 Days)** – Meetings with teachers, families, and stakeholders
  2. **Assessment Phase (30–60 Days)** – Identifying key strengths and gaps in student achievement
  3. **Action Phase (60–90 Days)** – Implementing first major initiative (aligned with district goals)

Step 4: Overcome Bias and Build Your Leadership Presence

Marginalized candidates often **face unconscious bias in hiring processes**—being **over-scrutinized, required to "prove" readiness, or dismissed for being "too ambitious"** (Macias & Stephens, 2019). Preparing with **strategic responses and confident storytelling** helps counteract these biases.

Actionable Steps:

✓ Anticipate Bias-Driven Questions – Be ready to **challenge coded language** (e.g., "Do you think you're ready for this?")
→ "MY EXPERIENCE LEADING DISTRICT-WIDE EQUITY INITIATIVES HAS PREPARED ME TO TAKE ON THIS ROLE SUCCESSFULLY.").
✓ Use the STAR Method – Structure responses with **Situation, Task, Action, and Result** to showcase your leadership impact.
✓ Present a 90-Day Leadership Entry Plan – Share a **strategic plan** outlining **your first three months in the role,** demonstrating **preparedness and vision.**

Example STAR Response for Leadership Readiness:

- **Situation:** AS AN ASSISTANT PRINCIPAL, I NOTICED INEQUITIES IN DISCIPLINE PRACTICES DISPROPORTIONATELY AFFECTING STUDENTS OF COLOR.

- **Task:** MY GOAL WAS TO IMPLEMENT RESTORATIVE JUSTICE PRACTICES AND REDUCE EXCLUSIONARY DISCIPLINE.

- **Action:** I PROVIDED PROFESSIONAL DEVELOPMENT TO TEACHERS, ENGAGED FAMILIES IN CONFLICT RESOLUTION STRATEGIES, AND DEVELOPED A SCHOOL-WIDE BEHAVIORAL INTERVENTION PLAN.
- **Result:** SUSPENSIONS DROPPED BY 40%, AND STUDENTS REPORTED AN IMPROVED SENSE OF BELONGING.

Actionable Strategies:
✓ **Be Assertive in Negotiations**

- Research salary benchmarks via **AASA's Superintendent Salary Report** and **state school leader databases**.
- If offered less than a **male or white counterpart** for the same role, **negotiate with confidence**:
   - "Based on my experience and market research, I believe a salary of [$X] is appropriate given my qualifications and impact."

✓ **Challenge the "Double Standard" Bias**

- Studies show **women and people of color face harsher scrutiny** in leadership roles.
- Strategy: Keep a **Leadership Impact Log** (a running list of data-driven successes) to counteract any **subjective evaluations**.

✓ **Use Visibility Strategies**

- Write **op-eds** on leadership and equity in education (published on **EdWeek, The 74,** or district blogs).
- Serve on **statewide or national advisory boards** (AERA, NAESP, NASSP).

✓ **Be Strategic About Career Pathing**

- **Do not stay in the same role too long** – research shows underrepresented leaders **wait longer for promotions**.
- Be **intentional about exit strategies** if a district does not value equity-focused leadership.

Step 5: Strengthen Your Leadership Network and Sponsorship

Marginalized leaders often walk a tightrope between advocacy and diplomacy—challenging inequities while navigating the politics of leadership (Jean-Marie et al., 2009).

Actionable Steps:
✓ Choose Strategic Moments for Advocacy – Learn when to **push for immediate change** vs. when to **build coalitions before acting**.
✓ Frame Advocacy with Data & Solutions – Use **data-driven insights** to advocate for equity-based policies.
✓ Leverage Your Network for Collective Action – Engage **other leaders, educators, and community stakeholders** to drive change together.

💡 **Advocacy in Action Example:**
Instead of saying: "OUR DISTRICT DOES NOT HIRE ENOUGH DIVERSE LEADERS."
Try: "OUR DISTRICT LEADERSHIP IS 80% WHITE, YET OUR STUDENT POPULATION IS 70% DIVERSE. I PROPOSE A DISTRICT-WIDE LEADERSHIP DEVELOPMENT PROGRAM FOCUSED ON PROMOTING TALENTED EDUCATORS OF COLOR INTO LEADERSHIP ROLES."

Actionable Strategies:

✅ **Secure a Leadership Sponsor (Not Just a Mentor)**

- **Mentors give advice. Sponsors create opportunities.**
- Identify **an influential leader** who can actively recommend you for promotions.
- Example: **Instead of "mentorship meetings," ask a sponsor to advocate for you** in hiring discussions.

✅ **Join Leadership Cohorts for Marginalized Leaders**

- **AASA Women in Leadership Initiative** (Superintendent pipeline support)
- **ALAS (Association of Latino Administrators & Superintendents)**
- **The Urban Leaders Fellowship** (Equity-focused leadership preparation)

✅ **Attend National Conferences and Present Your Expertise**

- Conferences where **hiring officials recruit future leaders**:
    - AASA's National Conference on Education
    - NAESP & NASSP Leadership Conferences
    - Voices $ Equity

✅ **Engage in Reverse Mentorship**

- Mentor **aspiring principals and leaders from underrepresented groups** to **build a future pipeline.**
- Research suggests **leaders who mentor others are more likely to receive promotions.**

Final Blueprint Task: Your Personal Equity-Driven Leadership Action Plan

At the end of this section, readers should draft a **Personal Leadership Action Plan** to **strategically navigate the leadership pipeline.** Use the following template:

📌 Personal Leadership Action Plan

1☐. **My Leadership Philosophy:** *(Summarize your leadership values and approach in 3–5 sentences.)*

2☐. **My Leadership Brand (3 Words):** _____ | _____ | _____

3☐. **My 5-Year Career Goal:** *(Clearly define your next leadership position goal.)*

4☐. **Immediate Steps to Reach It:** *(List 3 concrete steps to move toward your goal.)*
-
-
-

5☐. **Key Leadership Network(s) I Will Join:** *(List 2–3 professional organizations or cohorts to engage with.)*
-
-

6☐. **My Leadership Portfolio Assets:** *(List the key materials you will update: resume, letters of recommendation, media features, etc.)*
-
-

By **completing this plan,** you will have a **structured roadmap** to **break systemic barriers and secure leadership roles** in education.

You Belong in Leadership

The road to leadership for **marginalized leaders is not linear,** but with **intentional strategy, advocacy, and preparation,** you can **break through barriers and redefine leadership in education.** You do not **need permission to lead**—the **system needs** your perspective, skills, and **commitment to equity.**

"True succession planning embraces the spirit of the dandelion: resilient, inclusive, and thriving in diverse environments, spreading growth beyond traditional boundaries."

-Dr. LeAnne Salazar Montoya

Chapter 10
Spreading the Seeds
The Next Steps in Leadership

Chapter 10

Spreading the Seeds – The Next Steps in Leadership

The Collective Power of Leadership

Leadership is not about **reaching the finish line alone**—it is about **bringing others along, transforming systems, and creating sustainable change**. True leadership is **not just about individual success but about collective impact** (Kouzes & Posner, 2017).

For **marginalized leaders**, success is not measured by **titles or positions**, but by **how effectively we uplift others, break systemic barriers, and reshape leadership structures to be more inclusive** (Jean-Marie, Normore, & Brooks, 2009).

This final chapter will explore:
Encouragement and next steps for readers as they step into leadership roles
A call to action for systemic change in educational leadership
Resources and continued learning opportunities for lifelong growth
Warnings about toxic leadership behaviors—how to avoid Queen Bee Syndrome, Crab Syndrome, professional bullying, and exclusionary cliques

By the end of this chapter, you will be equipped with **next steps to expand your impact, foster inclusivity, and lead with collective strength**.

Encouragement and Next Steps for Readers

Stepping into leadership—especially as a **marginalized educator**—can be **both exhilarating and overwhelming**. You may face **barriers, resistance, and doubt**, but know this:

- You belong in leadership.
- Your voice matters.
- You are part of something bigger than yourself.

📖 Words from Resilient Leaders:
✓ "IF LEADERSHIP FEELS LONELY, FIND YOUR PEOPLE. BUILD A NETWORK OF LIKE-MINDED LEADERS WHO WILL SUPPORT YOU."
✓ "KEEP LEARNING, GROWING, AND LEADING. LEADERSHIP IS A JOURNEY, NOT A DESTINATION."
✓ "REMEMBER, NO ONE RISES ALONE. LIFT AS YOU CLIMB."

Action Steps to Keep Growing as a Leader:
Find a mentor – Reach out to experienced leaders for guidance.
Join a leadership network – Engage with **AASA, ALAS, NABSE, NAESP**, or other affinity groups.
Engage in professional development – Continue learning through **conferences, leadership programs, and coaching**.

A Call to Action for Systemic Change

Leadership is not just about **personal advancement**—it is about **transforming systems to create equity and opportunity for others.**

How Can You Be a Change Agent in Leadership?

✓ **Challenge hiring biases** – Advocate for **fair and transparent leadership selection processes** (Bailes & Guthery, 2020).
✓ **Push for mentorship and sponsorship programs** – Support **emerging leaders** to strengthen leadership pipelines (New Leaders, 2022).
✓ **Advocate for policy change** – Work with **school boards, districts, and legislators** to implement policies that **prioritize leadership diversity and inclusion** (Khalifa, 2018).

Key Research on Systemic Change in Leadership:
📖 **Khalifa, M. (2018).** CULTURALLY RESPONSIVE SCHOOL LEADERSHIP.

- Discusses **how school leaders can dismantle inequities and implement systemic change.**

📖 Bailes, L. P., & Guthery, S. (2020). HELD DOWN AND HELD BACK: SYSTEMATICALLY DELAYED PRINCIPAL PROMOTIONS BY RACE AND GENDER.

- Provides **evidence of systemic hiring biases** and strategies to **dismantle barriers for underrepresented leaders.**

📌 Action Step:
Identify one area where you can advocate for change in your school or district—then take the first step to make it happen.

What NOT to Do: Avoiding Toxic Leadership Behaviors

While **mentorship, inclusivity, and advocacy create strong leadership communities**, certain behaviors can **undermine progress and divide marginalized leaders.**

🚫 **The Queen Bee Syndrome** – THE BELIEF THAT THERE IS ONLY ROOM FOR ONE WOMAN OR MARGINALIZED LEADER AT THE TOP.
✓ **Solution:** Be a **connector, not a gatekeeper**—support other women and emerging leaders.

🚫 **The Crab Syndrome** – PULLING OTHERS DOWN INSTEAD OF LIFTING THEM UP, OFTEN DUE TO COMPETITION OR INTERNALIZED BIAS.
✓ **Solution: Celebrate others' success**—collective advancement strengthens all leaders.

🚫 **Professional Bullying** – SABOTAGING COLLEAGUES, SPREADING NEGATIVITY, OR UNDERMINING OTHERS' WORK.
✓ **Solution:** Lead with **integrity, collaboration, and emotional intelligence** (Goleman, 1998).

🚫 **Cliques That Exclude** – CREATING IN-GROUPS THAT ISOLATE OTHERS, PARTICULARLY MARGINALIZED VOICES.
✓ **Solution: Foster belonging**—true leadership is about inclusivity, not exclusivity.

Key Research on Toxic Leadership Behaviors:

📖 Eagly, A. H., & Carli, L. L. (2007). THROUGH THE LABYRINTH: THE TRUTH ABOUT HOW WOMEN BECOME LEADERS.

- Examines **why women sometimes resist supporting each other in leadership** and how to **foster collective advancement.**

📖 Goleman, D. (1998). WORKING WITH EMOTIONAL INTELLIGENCE.

- Explains how **leaders with high emotional intelligence foster collaboration and reduce workplace toxicity.**

📌 Action Step:
Commit to leading with inclusivity. Identify one way you can **support, uplift, and empower others in leadership spaces.**

Resources and Continued Learning

📚 Books for Leadership Development:

- **Kouzes, J. M., & Posner, B. Z. (2017).** THE LEADERSHIP CHALLENGE.

- **Collins, J. (2001).** GOOD TO GREAT: WHY SOME COMPANIES MAKE THE LEAP... AND OTHERS DON'T.

- **Edmondson, A. C. (2019).** THE FEARLESS ORGANIZATION: CREATING PSYCHOLOGICAL SAFETY IN THE WORKPLACE.

🎓 Leadership Development Programs:
✓ **AASA Women in Leadership Initiative** – Advocating for more women in superintendent roles.
✓ **ALAS Superintendent and Principal Leadership Academy** – Supporting Latino administrators.
✓ **NAESP Principals of Color Network** – Fostering leadership diversity in school leadership.

💻 Online Resources & Networks:
✓ **The Wallace Foundation** – Research on principal pipelines and leadership equity.
✓ **New Leaders** – Leadership training and mentorship for underrepresented educators.
✓ **Education Trust's Leadership Equity Resources** – Strategies for building diverse leadership pipelines.

📌 Action Step:
Choose one resource to explore further and commit to a professional development goal.

The Power of Collective Leadership

Leadership is not about **climbing alone**—it is about **bringing others with you and ensuring that the next generation has more opportunities than you did.**

Final Thoughts on Leadership:
- Alone, we are a single seed. Together, we are a field of dandelions—resilient, unbreakable, and unstoppable.
- The most successful leaders don't just lead—they create pathways for others to lead.
- Your leadership journey is just beginning—go forward, lift others, and continue to plant seeds of change.

What will be your leadership legacy? Write your leadership commitment statement and take action today.

The seeds have been planted—now go out and lead.

The Fields We Sow – Leadership, Legacy, and the Power of Representation

Leadership is not for the faint of heart. It requires **resilience, courage, and an unwavering commitment to impact.** It demands that we push through **barriers, bias, and bureaucracy** while holding onto the vision of a **better, more equitable future.** For too long, the pathways to leadership have been **guarded by gatekeepers and riddled with obstacles**—but we are not here to ask for permission. We are here to lead.

The journey of a marginalized leader is not easy. There will be those who **doubt you, dismiss you, or attempt to gaslight your experiences.** There will be moments of exhaustion, frustration, and questioning whether the fight is worth it. But the truth is this: **your leadership is necessary, your voice is powerful, and your presence changes everything.**

The impact of representation in leadership cannot be overstated.

- When a young girl sees a **woman of color leading a school district**, she realizes she, too, can lead.

- When a first-generation college student sees **a principal who shares their story**, they understand that education is their pathway forward.

- When a community sees **leaders who reflect their experiences, culture, and values**, trust is built, and transformation begins.

The **greatest victory of leadership** is not in holding a title but in **opening doors for others, creating opportunities, and challenging systems that were not designed for us to succeed.**

The Work is Not Done, But We Are Not Done Either

❦ **We are the dandelions that refuse to be uprooted.** We break through concrete barriers, take root in unexpected places, and spread seeds of change wherever the wind carries us.

❦ **We do not work in isolation.** Like an **army of ants**, we move together—lifting, supporting, and ensuring that no one is left behind.

❦ **We reject toxic leadership cycles.** We choose **inclusion over exclusion, collaboration over competition**, and **legacy over ego**.

The Future is Ours to Shape

To the leader stepping into their power—know this:

- **You belong at the table.** If the table excludes you, **build your own**.
- **You are not alone.** Find your allies, mentors, and co-conspirators in change.
- **Your leadership matters.** The impact you make today will ripple across generations.

The work is long, the obstacles are real, but the future is waiting for leaders like you.

So, rise. Lead boldly. Speak your truth. And remember—**the seeds you plant today will become the forests of tomorrow.**

Now, go. **Lead, uplift, and change the world.**

Appendices

Leadership Self-Assessment Tool

Instructions:
Reflect on your leadership qualities, strengths, and areas for growth. Use this self-assessment to identify where you are in your journey and what steps you can take to enhance your leadership skills.

Part 1: Leadership Strengths and Growth Areas

✓ **Rate Yourself on a Scale from 1-5** (1 = Needs Growth, 5 = Strength)

Leadership Quality	Rating (1-5)	Example from Your Experience
Vision and Strategic Thinking		
Communication and Public Speaking		
Conflict Resolution and Mediation		
Cultural Competence and Equity Leadership		
Decision-Making Under Pressure		
Team Building and Staff Development		
Emotional Intelligence and Self-Awareness		
Community and Stakeholder Engagement		
Change Management and Innovation		
Mentorship and Sponsorship of Others		

Part 2: Leadership Reflection Questions

- What are your **three strongest leadership qualities**?
- What are **two areas you want to improve in the next year**?
- How do you handle **adversity and conflict** in leadership?
- Who has **mentored or sponsored you**, and how has that shaped your journey?
- What is your **long-term leadership goal**?

Identify **one leadership skill** you want to develop further. Create a **plan to improve in this area** over the next six months.

Career Planning Template for Aspiring Leaders

Instructions:
Use this template to map out your leadership goals, steps for career advancement, and key milestones to track your progress.

Part 1: Defining Your Leadership Vision

My Leadership Why:
(EXAMPLE: "I WANT TO BECOME A PRINCIPAL TO CREATE EQUITABLE LEARNING ENVIRONMENTS AND MENTOR NEW TEACHERS.")

My Leadership Strengths:
1.
2.
3.

Areas I Want to Develop:
1.
2.
3.

Part 2: Career Path Planning

✓ **Where Are You Now?** (CURRENT POSITION: E.G., TEACHER, ASSISTANT PRINCIPAL, DISTRICT STAFF)
✓ **Where Do You Want to Be?** (SHORT-TERM GOAL: E.G., PRINCIPAL, DIRECTOR, SUPERINTENDENT)
✓ **Long-Term Leadership Goal:** (ULTIMATE CAREER ASPIRATION: E.G., STATE EDUCATION LEADER, SCHOOL BOARD MEMBER, POLICY ADVOCATE)

Part 3: Action Steps for Career Growth

Goal	Timeline	Steps to Take	Support Needed
Obtain leadership certification	6 months	Enroll in certification program, complete coursework	Funding, mentorship
Build a professional network	Ongoing	Join leadership organizations, attend conferences	Find a mentor or sponsor
Gain experience in leadership roles	1 year	Apply for committee positions, lead initiatives	Support from current leadership

Action Step: Identify **one immediate step** you can take in the next month to move closer to your leadership goal.

Practice Interview Questions

Vision & Leadership Style

1. What is your leadership philosophy, and how do you ensure it aligns with the mission and vision of an educational institution?

2. How do you foster a culture of innovation, equity, and inclusion within a school district or educational organization?

3. Describe a time when you had to lead an organization through a major transition or crisis. What steps did you take, and what was the outcome?

Strategic Planning & Decision-Making

4. How do you approach strategic planning in education? Can you provide an example of a successful initiative you led?

5. What data-driven decision-making processes do you use to improve student achievement and organizational success?

6. How do you handle competing priorities when making budgetary and resource allocation decisions?

Equity, Diversity, and Inclusion

7. What strategies have you implemented to close achievement gaps and support historically marginalized students?

8. How do you recruit, retain, and support a diverse team of educators and administrators?

9. What steps would you take to ensure that policies and practices are equitable for all students, particularly those from underrepresented communities?

Stakeholder Engagement & Communication

10. How do you build and maintain trust with key stakeholders, including teachers, parents, community members, and board members?

11. Describe a situation where you had to navigate conflict between different groups within a school or district. How did you resolve it?

12. What communication strategies do you use to effectively convey your vision and goals to a diverse audience?

Talent Development & Organizational Culture

13. How do you identify and develop future leaders within your organization?

14. What role does coaching and mentoring play in your leadership approach, and how do you implement it within a school system?

15. How do you foster a culture of continuous professional learning and growth among educators and staff?

Your Leadership Journey Begins Today

You have the tools, knowledge, and vision—now it's time to take action. Use these worksheets as your **personal roadmap** to build your leadership profile, plan your career path, and connect with resources that will empower your growth.

Next Step: Take one action today—whether it's reaching out to a mentor, joining a professional group, or setting a leadership goal. Your leadership matters, and the future needs YOU.

10 Takeaways: The Dandelion's Journey and the Struggle of Marginalized Leaders

The **dandelion** is often overlooked, underestimated, and even seen as a nuisance. Yet, **it persists, adapts, and thrives in conditions where others cannot**. This resilience mirrors the journey of **marginalized leaders**, who must break through systemic barriers, withstand adversity, and carve pathways for future generations.

1. Pushing Through Concrete – Breaking Systemic Barriers
Dandelions push through cracks in the concrete, thriving in hostile environments where they weren't expected to grow.
Marginalized leaders often face systemic barriers in leadership pipelines, including bias in hiring, limited mentorship, and resistance to change. Yet, they persist and create spaces for themselves, proving that leadership belongs to everyone—not just a select few.

2. Roots That Run Deep – Staying Grounded in Identity
Dandelions have deep, unshakable roots, allowing them to survive harsh conditions and regrow even after being cut down.
Marginalized leaders face microaggressions, pushback, and professional setbacks—but their strength comes from deeply rooted cultural heritage, lived experiences, and an unshakable sense of purpose. Staying true to their values and identity fuels their ability to lead with authenticity.

3. Adaptability and Resilience – Thriving Despite the Odds
Dandelions grow in almost any soil—from city sidewalks to untouched meadows. Their adaptability is key to their survival.
Marginalized leaders must be adaptable, navigating institutional politics, bias, and shifting expectations while remaining true to their mission. Their resilience allows them to turn obstacles into opportunities for growth.

4. Multiplying, Not Just Surviving – Expanding Leadership Opportunities
One dandelion releases thousands of seeds, ensuring that its presence spreads far and wide.
True leadership is not just about personal success—it's about creating opportunities for others. Marginalized leaders mentor, sponsor, and advocate for systemic changes that uplift the next generation. They ensure that their impact reaches beyond their own career.

5. Often Misunderstood and Undervalued – Challenging Stereotypes
Dandelions are often dismissed as weeds, despite being nutrient-rich, medicinally valuable, and essential to the ecosystem.
Marginalized leaders are often undervalued or questioned in ways that their majority counterparts are not. Assumptions about competence, leadership style, or "readiness" create unnecessary hurdles—but like the dandelion, they prove their worth through action and excellence.

6. A Source of Strength and Healing – Transformational Leadership

Dandelions have medicinal properties, known for their ability to detoxify, heal, and restore balance. Marginalized leaders bring necessary transformation to educational spaces, challenging inequities, advocating for students, and creating inclusive environments that uplift entire communities. Their leadership is a force for healing and systemic change.

7. Finding Strength in the Wind – Using Challenges to Spread Impact

Dandelions depend on the wind to scatter their seeds, turning an external force into an opportunity for expansion.

Marginalized leaders turn challenges into stepping stones. Instead of being discouraged by adversity, they use their experiences to become stronger, advocate more effectively, and reach new leadership heights.

8. Blooming Where Others Cannot – Leading in Uncharted Spaces

Dandelions flourish in places where other flowers struggle, proving that beauty and strength can emerge from unexpected places.

Marginalized leaders often find themselves as the "first" or "only" in leadership spaces. Despite facing isolation and high expectations, they make an impact where others have not dared to lead.

9. Collective Power – Leadership is Stronger Together

A single dandelion can spread seeds across an entire field, transforming empty spaces into vibrant ecosystems.

Marginalized leaders succeed when they support one another. Instead of competing for limited leadership spaces, they lift each other up, mentor emerging leaders, and advocate collectively. Alone, the impact is small, but together, they create movements.

10. The Cycle of Growth – Leaving a Leadership Legacy

Dandelions don't just bloom once. Their seeds ensure that the next generation thrives, long after the original plant is gone.

True leadership is about legacy. Marginalized leaders don't just fight for themselves—they fight for those who come after them. They work to break cycles of exclusion, create equitable leadership pipelines, and ensure that future leaders don't have to struggle the same way.

Embracing the Dandelion Mindset in Leadership

The dandelion is not fragile—it is unstoppable.

It pushes through concrete.

It spreads where it is least expected.

It survives storms and finds strength in the wind.

It transforms barren spaces into fields of possibility.

Marginalized leaders are no different.

Every challenge, every closed door, every moment of doubt is another crack in the concrete that allows growth.

The seeds of leadership are already within you—it's time to let them take root, flourish, and spread.

About the Author

Dr. LeAnne Salazar Montoya is a seasoned leadership coach, educator, and advocate dedicated to guiding the next generation of school leaders, particularly those from marginalized backgrounds. A first-generation scholar from rural New Mexico, she has spent over two decades in education, rising from classroom teacher to district-level leadership and now serving as an assistant professor on the tenure track at the University of Nevada, Las Vegas (UNLV) in the Educational Leadership Department.

With advanced degrees from New Mexico State University and the University of New Mexico, Dr. Montoya's expertise spans leadership development, policy, and equity in education. Her research and practice emphasize creating pathways for underrepresented leaders, advocating for women in education, and fostering inclusive leadership practices that reflect the diverse communities and schools serve.

Throughout her career, Dr. Montoya has worked with aspiring leaders, mentoring them to break barriers, challenge systemic inequities, and step into leadership with confidence and purpose. As the chair of the National Professional Learning, Growth, and Development Committee for the Association of Latino Administrators and Superintendents (ALAS) and an officer for the American Educational Research Association (AERA) Superintendency Special Interest Group (SIG), and Research on Women in Education (RWE) she collaborates with leaders nationwide to bridge research and practice in educational leadership.

Her leadership philosophy is deeply rooted in the resilience of the dandelion—an unassuming yet powerful force that thrives despite adversity, spreads its seeds of knowledge and inspiration, and creates new opportunities for growth. DANDELION DIARIES is the culmination of her life's work: a blueprint for marginalized leaders who aspire to school leadership positions, equipping them with the strategies, insights, and confidence needed to navigate the path to leadership. She has also curated and founded the Radiance Project, a series of anthologies intended to inspire and encourage aspiring leaders.

Through her writing, research, and mentorship, Dr. Montoya continues to champion the belief that leadership is not just about reaching the top—it's about lifting others along the way, planting seeds of change, and cultivating a future where leadership reflects the strength and diversity of the communities it serves. At this stage of her career it is about IMPACT and a call to action for the leadership pipeline to be more representative of the populations they serve.

References

AASA – The School Superintendents Association. (2023). The time is now: A playbook for women in educational leadership. Retrieved from www.aasa.org

Bailes, L. P., & Guthery, S. (2020). Held down and held back: Systematically delayed principal promotions by race and gender. AERA Open, 6(2), 1-17. https://doi.org/10.1177/2332858420929298

Bass, B. M. (1990). From transactional to transformational leadership: Learning to share the vision. Organizational Dynamics, 18(3), 19-31.

Bass, B. M., & Riggio, R. E. (2006). Transformational leadership (2nd ed.). Lawrence Erlbaum Associates.

Brown, A. L. (2012). On human kinds and role models: A critical discussion about the African American male teacher. Educational Researcher, 41(3), 89-95. https://doi.org/10.3102/0013189X12436699

Bryk, A. S., & Schneider, B. (2002). Trust in schools: A core resource for improvement. Russell Sage Foundation.

Bryk, A. S., Sebring, P. B., Allensworth, E., Luppescu, S., & Easton, J. Q. (2010). Organizing schools for improvement: Lessons from Chicago. University of Chicago Press.

Clance, P. R., & Imes, S. A. (1978). The imposter phenomenon in high achieving women: Dynamics and therapeutic intervention. Psychotherapy: Theory, Research & Practice, 15(3), 241-247. https://doi.org/10.1037/h0086006

Collins, J. (2001). Good to great: Why some companies make the leap… and others don't. HarperCollins.

Coombs, W. T. (2014). Ongoing crisis communication: Planning, managing, and responding (4th ed.). SAGE Publications.

Eagly, A. H., & Carli, L. L. (2007). Through the labyrinth: The truth about how women become leaders. Harvard Business Review Press.

Edmondson, A. C. (2019). The fearless organization: Creating psychological safety in the workplace for learning, innovation, and growth. Wiley.

Fullan, M. (2014). Leading in a culture of change (2nd ed.). Wiley.

Fuller, E. J., & Young, M. D. (2022). Challenges and opportunities in diversifying the leadership pipeline: Flow, leaks, and interventions. Leadership and Policy in Schools, 21(4), 1–20. https://doi.org/10.1080/15700763.2021.1976156

Goddard, R. D., Hoy, W. K., & Woolfolk Hoy, A. (2000). Collective teacher efficacy: Its meaning, measure, and impact on student achievement. American Educational Research Journal, 37(2), 479–507.

Goleman, D. (1998). Working with emotional intelligence. Bantam Books.

Grogan, M., & Shakeshaft, C. (2011). Women and educational leadership. Jossey-Bass.

Heifetz, R. A., & Linsky, M. (2002). Leadership on the line: Staying alive through the dangers of leading. Harvard Business Review Press.

Heifetz, R., Grashow, A., & Linsky, M. (2009). The practice of adaptive leadership: Tools and tactics for changing your organization and the world. Harvard Business Review Press.

hooks, b. (1994). Teaching to transgress: Education as the practice of freedom. Routledge.

Ibarra, H., Carter, N. M., & Silva, C. (2010). Why men still get more promotions than women. Harvard Business Review, 88(9), 80–85.

Ishimaru, A. M. (2019). Just schools: Building equitable collaborations with families and communities. Teachers College Press.

Jean-Marie, G. (2008). Leadership for social justice: Preparing 21st-century school leaders. Journal of Research on Leadership Education, 3(1), 1–31.

Jean-Marie, G., Normore, A. H., & Brooks, J. S. (2009). Leadership for social justice: Preparing 21st-century school leaders. Journal of Research on Leadership Education, 4(1), 1–31.

Khalifa, M. (2018). Culturally responsive school leadership. Harvard Education Press.

Khalifa, M., Gooden, M. A., & Davis, J. E. (2016). Culturally responsive school leadership: A synthesis of the literature. Review of Educational Research, 86(4), 1272–1311. https://doi.org/10.3102/0034654316630383

Kirtman, L. (2013). Leadership and teams: The missing piece of the educational reform puzzle. Pearson.

Kouzes, J. M., & Posner, B. Z. (2017). The leadership challenge: How to make extraordinary things happen in organizations (6th ed.). Jossey-Bass.

Kram, K. E. (1985). Mentoring at work: Developmental relationships in organizational life. University Press of America.

Ladson-Billings, G. (1995). Toward a theory of culturally relevant pedagogy. American Educational Research Journal, 32(3), 465–491.

Macias, A., & Stephens, S. (2019). Intersectionality in the field of education: A critical look at race, gender, treatment, pay, and leadership. Journal of Latinos and Education, 18(1), 46-64. https://doi.org/10.1080/15348431.2017.1383912

Maslach, C., & Leiter, M. P. (2016). Burnout: The cost of caring. Malor Books.

Méndez-Morse, S. (2004). Latina school leaders: Challenges and strengths. Journal of Women in Educational Leadership, 2(4), 271-283.

Miller, P., & Garran, P. (2017). Bias and hiring in educational leadership: A review. Journal of School Leadership, 27(4), 552-580.

New Leaders. (2022). The shoulder tap: Educators of color on the leadership representation gap and what we can do about it. Retrieved from www.newleaders.org

Shakeshaft, C. (1987). Women in educational administration. Sage.

Stone, D., Patton, B., & Heen, S. (2010). Difficult conversations: How to discuss what matters most. Penguin Books.

Tallerico, M. (2000). Accessing the superintendency: The unwritten rules. Corwin Press.

The Wallace Foundation. (2021). How principals affect students and schools: A systematic synthesis of two decades of research. Retrieved from www.wallacefoundation.org

Ury, W. (1991). Getting past no: Negotiating in difficult situations. Bantam Books.

Made in the USA
Las Vegas, NV
26 March 2025